MANAGING
YOUR
FAMILY BUSINESS

by Marshall W. Northington, Ph.D.

THE
CRISP
SMALL BUSINESS &
ENTREPRENEURSHIP
SERIES

CREDITS

Editor: Janis Paris

Layout/Design: ExecuStaff

Cover Design: Kathleen Gadway

Library of Congress 92-54372
ISBN-1-56052-174-0

Limits of Liability and Disclaimer of Warranty

The author and publisher have used their best efforts in preparing this book and make no warranty of any kind, expressed or implied, with regard to the instructions and suggestions contained herein. This book is not intended to render legal or accounting advice. Such advice should be obtained from competent, licensed professionals.

INTRODUCTION TO THE SERIES

This series of books is intended to inform and assist those of you who are in the beginning stages of starting a new small business venture or who are considering such an undertaking.

It is because you are confident of your abilities that you are taking this step. These books will provide additional information and support along the way.

Not every new business will succeed. The more information you have about budgeting, cash flow management, accounts receivable, and marketing and employee management, the better prepared you will be for the inevitable pitfalls.

A unique feature of the Crisp Small Business & Entrepreneurship Series is the personal involvement exercises, which give you many opportunities to apply immediately the concepts presented to your own business.

In each book in the series, these exercises take the form of "Your Turn," a checklist to confirm your understanding of the concept just presented and "Ask Yourself," a series of chapter-ending questions designed to evaluate your overall understanding or commitment.

In addition, numerous case studies are included, and each book is cross-referenced to others in the series and to other publications.

BOOKS IN THE SERIES

▶ **Operating a Really Small Business**
Betty M. Bivins

▶ **Budgeting: A Primer for Entrepreneurs**
Terry Dickey

▶ **Getting a Business Loan: Your Step-By-Step Guide**
Orlando J. Antonini

▶ **Nobody Gets Rich Working for Somebody Else:**
An Entrepreneur's Guide
Roger Fritz

▶ **Marketing Strategies for Small Businesses**
Richard F. Gerson, Ph.D.

▶ **Financial Basics for Small Business Success**
James O. Gill

▶ **Extending Credit and Collecting Cash:**
A Small Business Guide
Lynn Harrison

▶ **Avoiding Mistakes in Your New Business**
David Karlson, Ph.D.

▶ **Buying Your First Franchise:**
The Least You Need to Know
Rebecca Luhn, Ph.D.

▶ **Buying a Business: Tips for the First-Time Buyer**
Ronald J. McGregor

▶ **Your New Business: A Personal Plan for Success**
Charles L. Martin, Ph.D.

▶ **Managing the Family Business: A Guide for Success**
Marshall W. Northington, Ph.D.

▶ **The Female Entrepreneur**
Connie Sitterly, Ed.D.

ACKNOWLEDGEMENTS

This book couldn't have been written without the help of some very special people in my life. They were tolerant, sensitive and understanding of what this meant to me.

No one deserves greater recognition than Linda, who gave up time, and sometimes peace of mind, to assist with editing, typing and proofreading. Without her help to clear my head, this could have been a tortuous task.

To Chelsea and Kate, who missed me on Saturdays, Sundays and some evenings, I extend my heartfelt gratitude for their tolerance and acceptance. Now I promise to make up for lost time.

CONTENTS

CONTENTS (continued)

PREFACE

I got into the family-owned business consulting profession in an interesting way. When my father died, he left a thriving, growing insulation business to my mother. She had little experience in this business and was soon overwhelmed. I was thousands of miles away and not much help. Finally, after a while, in her interest I felt it was necessary to join the company and delay opening my counseling psychology practice. My plan was to work with the company for a few years, start a practice and be a resource to the family regarding business issues.

This book is about what I learned. All over the country, family businesses are productive, profitable and sustaining. Sometimes this flow is interrupted by family problems. The dimensions this might take are presented in this book.

I have written from a counselor's point of view. Family business problems reflect what is going on in all families. I do a fair amount of marriage counseling—trying to find a wellspring of equity in the family workplace for husbands and wives. Sons, daughters and other relatives are often a source of stress at the job. Finding a way through these problems, and sometimes suggesting a change, is part of my job. The rest is up to the client.

The most important area of my learning has been in succession planning. I've seen family businesses that don't recover after the death of the founder—because ideas for the ongoing operation of the firm were never made public.

There is no substitute for planning—everyone can benefit if the future is considered.

I believe that if I can change a person's view of the world by just a little, everything else will look different. Even the slightest alteration can bring serenity and satisfaction. Give it a chance.

CHAPTER
ONE

IS FAMILY
BUSINESS
FOR ME?

FINDING OUT IF A FAMILY BUSINESS IS RIGHT FOR YOU

An 11 P.M. phone call can mean a lot of things—and most of them are bad. Fighting through the fog of sleep, I answered my phone hoping it wasn't someone with a crisis.

Well . . . it was, and it wasn't. It was my friend and associate Dr. Ben Johnson. He had taken a call from an old classmate, Robert, who needed some help with a family and personal problem. Ben recommended that Robert set up an appointment with me. My friend presented a brief outline of Robert's problem: Robert's father, Allen, had recently passed away, leaving the family cabinet-making business to be managed by his mother, Grace, who didn't have a clue how to run it. Grace had called several times since the funeral to ask for assistance. Most of the time this required that Robert, with little or no knowledge of the issues, meet with the general manager to make decisions. All these demands were causing Robert a great deal of stress, and his wife thought a professional could help him.

Robert's experiences are not unusual. These days 80% of businesses in America are family owned, and 50% of all employment is in small, family-owned businesses. It isn't surprising that, more and more, family enterprises are seeking professional assistance to help solve business and family problems.

Until a few years ago, most business training was oriented toward large corporations that required sophisticated approaches to business management, sales and growth strategies. Massive amounts of research dollars have gone into learning about large corporations. By comparison, family businesses are vaguely understood. Only limited efforts by a few colleges and universities have produced insight into families working together in their own business.

Family Businesses and Stress

The family business leader is never just an employee. An entrepreneur takes on many risks to develop an independent and thriving business, but often this aspect is never articulated to the spouse or children, and they are often not prepared to handle these stresses.

A unique dimension of these enterprises is the emotional component. Conflicting personalities are forced to maintain a calm and pleasant and this effort over time, produces stress and anxiety. Finding a middle ground for behavior and emotions is sometimes difficult.

Yet, the emotional aspect of families in business is almost never discussed in professional or academic literature. It is an important issue, which if handled with sensitivity and understanding, can enable families in business to succeed. A family-owned business can provide a field for creativity, experimentation and expression. Where family members cooperate, the outcome is impressive.

Providing for family members can be achieved only through planning, prudent business practices and, most importantly, by building bridges to all family members who have a stake in the business's success.

Family business members are bound to one another by their mutually dependence on the success of the family enterprise. It is best not to be surprised by conflict. All families have discord; however, this doesn't mean these relationships are necessarily dysfunctional.

Making the Decision

Robert's problem was frustrating and urgent. In most cases, people take years to make the decision to open a business. In the meantime, they prepare by saving and talking it over with friends. Robert's decision had to be immediate—but yours can take more time. The tests and discussions included in this chapter should help you make this decision in the same way they helped Robert.

In his will, Allen left 50% of the company to his wife Grace and the remainder in equal shares to the three children: Robert, Steve and Janis. Wayne, the general manager, was working with a local bank to finance a buyout. Robert had heard his father complain about Wayne's personality and wasn't sure that Wayne would be a relief or source of stress to his mother.

Robert realized that, because of his father's illness, the business had lost market share the past few years. The region was economically depressed, which would make it difficult to sell the business for a profit. Robert was concerned that if his mother sold her shares of stock to Wayne, she would always be apprehensive about Wayne's ability to make her monthly payments. If the financial obligation to Grace couldn't be met, it may require her children to support their mother financially for some time. She was also worried about what kind of relationship her children would have with the company if Wayne was in control.

Is It for You? A Questionnaire

Robert knew that if he wanted to buy the business, he must secure his mother's share of the stock and make some arrangement with his brother and sister to carry out his intent to control the company. He realized that if he made this move, his personal family finances would change dramatically, and he would have to relocate his family to a city 125 miles away from their current home. Rachael, his wife, pledged her support without knowing what to expect. The basic concerns they addressed are presented here in question form.

What Owning a Business Would Mean to the Family: Discussion Questions

1. Would a spouse have to find a job to help pay day-to-day expenses?

2. Would it be a good idea for a spouse to work in the business with you?

3. How would your children react to a change that took them to a new city and new friends?

4. How would the physical proximity to family members affect you?

5. Would ownership of a company interfere in relationships with siblings, especially if financial concerns become an issue?

6. Would your standard of living be reduced to the extent that you may never again have the nice things you are used to?

7. How sure are you that this move would lead to prosperity?

8. Is this a good enough risk to pledge all your savings and future earnings?

Your Turn

Answer the following:

▶ Is your situation similar to Robert's? Which of Robert's family's basic concerns are also a concern to you and your family in taking over a family business?

▶ What other concerns affect your decision to take over a family business?

These considerations forced Robert to take a hard look at the situation. After lengthy family discussions, they decided to make a purchase offer to his mother for her stock. For now, his brother and sister wanted to maintain their stock in the company and trusted Robert to do the right thing to protect their interests. Robert and Rachel's concern was how to preserve their relationship through the expected rough times ahead. Their commitment to one another was strong, but they feared the unknown. Robert wanted to go through with the decision, but anxiety left him sleepless.

Robert knew about business from his experience as a loan officer at a statewide bank. When considering owning his own business, he told himself that it couldn't be any more difficult than what he was now doing. But if this was true, why did he still feel so unsettled about the decision he was making?

ASK YOURSELF

► How will you handle the special circumstances of beginning or taking over a family business?

► What are the expectations of the rest of your family about how the business will survive?

CHAPTER
TWO

THE
ENTREPRENEURIAL
PERSONALITY

DO YOU HAVE THE RIGHT STUFF?

With all the considerations in making the decision to start or take over a family business, the process can become confusing. One way to aid in the decision making is to explore your wants, desires, abilities and interests through standardized tests, which can help you learn if you have the talent and background for business management. This may be especially important if your education or experience is in a field not related to the family business or you question your ability to own or manage your own business. Psychologists and many counselors are qualified and experienced in administering these tests. Their analysis can provide you with the needed feedback about assuming a role in the family business.

Though many people doubt the value of testing, remember that the results of this process must be viewed as only one factor in your decision. The test itself will not tell you what to do. Used with other means, such as discussions with professionals and support of immediate family, tests can help to point out personal and professional strengths and weaknesses

Your Turn

Consult the Yellow Pages for counseling professionals experienced in career testing. They should be listed as psychologists, psychometrists or counselors with testing services. Call them and discuss your interest in their services. Ask them to describe the testing instruments they use, the time to administer them, follow-up meetings to present the results and fee schedule. The results should help you better understand yourself—you might even have fun—and enable you to make the best decisions for you and your family.

Robert decided to take a simple test of my own design, combined with a few standardized tests before he went too far with his purchase of his mother's cabinet company. We agreed that this approach would save a lot of time and money should he decide not to buy. Should purchasing be the right move, he would rest more confidently with his plan.

THE PERSONAL CONSIDERATION TEST

The personal consideration test, while not a scientific instrument, is reliable in specific circumstances. I designed it to force a choice with questions identifying areas of concern of men and women who desire to own their own business. I've included the test at the end of Chapter One for you to test your own reactions to important issues of family business ownership. If you have significantly more "Yes" answers than "No," you may have an entrepreneurial profile.

Robert's responses to the test questions showed that his attitude and level of commitment about working for himself were significant enough to encourage him. He scored high on the "enterprising" scales of the Strong Interest Inventory, which compares a person's interests with those of people already employed in specific occupations. This was supported by the Personal-Career Development Profile, sometimes called the 16 Personality Factor Questionnaire. This test measures for functionally independent and meaningful personality dimensions. These instruments, available for 40 years, have been useful for individual and group counseling. In this case they served to identify Robert's career interests and pointed to suitable personality characteristics for an entrepreneurial venture.

In my practice I've found that tests are also of great value when a family makes the decision to bring a relative into the family business or plans for a successor.

EXAMPLE

A Second Case Example

Bill, a local trucking owner, was concerned about his son's future in the family business. His son Frank, then 27, seemed to be stuck in the warehouse and delivery units of the company and showed no real desire or promise to do more than manual labor. Bill, at 57, was beginning to think about retirement and what to do with his company. He felt apprehensive about his son's ability to take over. Bill's wife was pressuring him to make a decision so she could enjoy Bill's retirement.

Bill, of course, received little feedback from Frank, who was usually on the road or with his girlfriend. A hand injury temporarily put Frank in the office, and he began to perceive that a future of driving may not be the only option available. Bill asked me to talk to Frank and assess his ability to move into management.

Frank took a personality test, a career interest test and the Personal Consider-ations Questionnaire in this book. The results revealed that:

a. Frank exhibited traits and characteristics common among successful business owners. Frank's management potential was easy to recognize.

b. Frank's relationship with his father had been suppressing his potential. He wanted to advance in the business, but felt his father was standing in his way by being too critical and withholding valuable job experiences.

Frank was gratified that the tests showed he had many important business-related qualities. When I met with Bill, he was elated:"This is what I needed to know." We discussed what training Frank needed and set guidelines for when Frank and Bill could accomplish them. Bill left smiling.

A month later Bill called. He said he couldn't be happier. I learned that Bill's chief field operations supervisor had suddenly quit, and Bill had decided to try Frank at this position. All Frank had needed was a chance. With a new job and additional pay, he was going to be married—much to his mother's delight.

Family Businesses Are Not for Everyone

Testing can also help people to decide if starting a family business is for them. Esther wanted to know if it would be a good idea for her to finance her son-in-law in a custom-home construction business. Her daughter, Karen, had been married to Hugh for two years. Hugh was an electrician and Karen an accountant with a local firm. Together they made a good, but not exorbitant, living and had a new home and automobiles. Both in their mid-twenties, they didn't anticipate having children for a few more years.

I asked Esther about Hugh's plans to start his own company. She said that he never talked about it, but she didn't see how he could remain an electrician forever. I felt Esther was trying to manipulate Hugh in her daughter's interest and agreed to see Hugh only if he would initiate the call for an appointment.

Hugh called, and we scheduled time during the following week. Hugh laughed when I explained my reluctance to see him. He said it was all right, he knew what Esther wanted and didn't mind going through the testing if it would help settle the matter. Hugh assured me that he was not interested in working for himself. He liked eight-hour days, vacations and not taking his work home with him at night. Besides, he and his wife had decided that when they had children, they wouldn't sacrifice their enjoyment by spending too much time on the job. His wife thought that her father had committed too much of his life to his business, contributing to his early death.

The test results showed that Hugh didn't demonstrate the desire nor aspiration of entrepreneurs, and his personality required an explicit job description and schedule much like his current job. Hugh felt relieved that his personality profile matched what he was doing so well. When I talked to Esther she at first grew pensive, then admitted that she was glad her daughter married a man who knew what he wanted.

A man with less maturity might have taken Esther up on her offer. If not for the aid of the tests, she might have been persistent enough to push Hugh into something he really didn't want, possibly harming her daughter's marriage.

Personality Patterns of Entrepreneurs

The common denominator for Robert and Calvin was that both men, in their employment histories, had worked for someone else. They were both competent or even exceptional employees. However, their experiences rarely allowed them to witness or participate in business management or planning. They were asked to perform in limited ways. Robert helped his clients by processing their loan applications. He told them how to structure a business plan for loan repayment that would be acceptable to his supervisor. He rarely made the final decision and was required to carry out the directives of his superiors.

Breaking Past the Limitations of Prior Jobs

Calvin, as a production engineer, was responsible for only one small part of the manufacturing and assembly process and had little exposure to the beginning or end product. Though he was aware of how the production schedule worked, his expertise was confined to one factor in the production scheme.

Both had limited experience with hiring and supervising employees. Robert had a secretary and an assistant, but both had passed a thorough screening process before they were interviewed by him. Blair had a large staff, but almost all the employees under his control were provided by the union, and he only had to talk with the shop steward to resolve problems. His secretary, like Robert's, was from the personnel office.

In all their experiences on the job, neither had given much thought to negotiating employment benefit packages, including major medical or liability insurance needs. Nor had they been required to knock on customer's doors looking for a payment. They worked their eight or nine hours, took three weeks vacation per year and had periodic raises. Now they both reflected enthusiasm, commitment to whatever it might take to succeed and a sense of making the decision to own a business not only for themselves, but for their families.

Once the Decision Is Made

Robert and Calvin fit many of the personality components of family business owners. They were willing to risk their savings in order to put themselves in business. In addition, they had a spirit brought out only in such situations. Once they decided what they wanted, it became a matter of *how* to do it—not whether it could be done. They were aware of the odds against them, but were committed to whatever was needed for success. They were also willing to set their fear of failure aside while they put all their energy into their business ventures.

Are You Compelled?

Robert and Calvin felt compelled to enter the business because, if they had not, they would have forever wondered if it was possible to "make it" in their own enterprise. They had opportunity, tools, personality and the right frame of mind. Their journey isn't uncommon.

Important Psychological Factors in Entrepreneurial Success

Success in family business doesn't occur by accident. Most entrepreneurs have learned their craft from someone else. Through experience on the job a person develops their approach and outlook.

The process of preparedness comes over time. An entrepreneur knows that with success comes profitability. Once he or she realizes it is possible to be faster, more efficient, more service-oriented than competitors, there are few roadblocks to trying.

Dedication, commitment and sheer force of character are aspects of this personality. Other traits include expertise, independence, social and professional skills, and risk taking. All the personality characteristics are intertwined and a person in business for him or herself will manifest almost all of them.

If you are contemplating going into business for yourself, consider each of these characteristics as independent values and then take them together as a whole. Only with the integration of these important factors can there be a reasonable hope for success.

Your Turn

Rate yourself as to your identification with each of the following factors:

▶ Are you confident about your readiness to strike out on your own?

▶ Do you prefer to work alone or with others?

▶ Do you feel confident that you can start your own business and retain control?

▶ Are you skilled enough working with people to evaluate them as important workers in your effort?

▶ Are you willing to pledge important assets in order to finance your venture?

If you are positive in your responses, you have a good chance of succeeding at your own business. These characteristics won't override the planning needed to organize your business, but the two in combination are potent.

I told Robert I thought it might be helpful to examine how entrepreneurs and other business people like himself reached the position they now enjoy. Personal attitudes about work require specific personality characteristics essential to family business success. These traits, in interaction with one another, produce a profile common to all successful business people.

Entrepreneurs Are Experts at What They Do

Family businesses frequently start out with an employee who has decided he or she knows as much as the boss. The reason for making a change may be the need to work independently, the loss of a previous job or the feeling that "I can do this job better on my own." Once confidence truly emerges and the person believes "I know what I'm doing," the desire to make improvements in the field of expertise make it difficult to say "no." The level of competence in this individual is matched only by the competition. Now, after all the years developing and growing an enterprise, an entrepreneur's command of the field is demonstrated by stature in the industry.

Family Business Owners are Fiercely Independent

Family business owners are fiercely independent. After all the sacrifices of bringing a business to its present success, they will not give up management control without a great deal of thought. They do it their way—that is part of their appeal. Decisions about how to handle customer relations, policy about how and who to hire, and strategy to expand market share are all shaped by the independent character of the family business owner.

Ability to Evaluate Others

Choosing the right people to keep a business running is essential to success. The ability to evaluate others is key to family business management. Every family business owner should have this attribute. In many cases, it is the talent for identifying a skill or an attitude unrecognized by others. Bringing new workers along until they can contribute is a tremendous asset to the family business owner. This kind of vision, along with a well-organized training program, can vastly improve a work situation.

Willing to Risk Everything

Almost all family business owners have had to make decisions that put their families and personal resources at risk. Faith that they can succeed makes risk taking a natural step. Signing personal guarantees and pledging their homes to cover a credit line are common for family business owners.

Family Business Owners Get the Job Done

Getting the task done when expected is job one of the entrepreneur. These are not 9-to-5 people. They usually open the office in the morning and are the last to leave at night. They are self starters. No one has to tell them what to do or when to do it. They work at their job all the time. This person willingly accepts responsibility for actions. These are men and women who have the vision for what it takes to succeed and will allow no compromise.

Beware of Becoming Authoritarian

Success breeds success. After so many years of profitability, family business owners and entrepreneurs tend to become complacent with their achievements. This shift is a very subtle, but endangering, outcome of success. While people around the owner can see the process taking place, the owner-manager often fails to notice that technology, product, management theory, market place and so on have changed. When business remains profitable, the owner sees no need to change style or methods in making business decisions. This is the basis for an authoritarian personality.

This personality type will not accept a broad range of choices due to the reliability of past decisions. If a method of inventory control has worked for the past 20 years, why look at any way to streamline or keep better accounting now? An authoritarian owner fears change. They are the owners who are reluctant to give up control to a younger manager unless forced by ill health or death—because no one else could do it better than they could.

For the employees of such a person, the potential for making inroads in the business are remote. Any attempt to help authoritarian owners overcome their fear of change will be met with roadblocks. They know how to do everything. Don't rock the boat and ruin a good thing . . . or leave.

Dealing with an Authoritarian Personality

If you find yourself in a family business that has a founder or owner with an authoritarian personality, making changes will be a challenge. Consider:

1. Establish very early on in your employment that you want an active role in decision making and problem solving. Then, in small increments, practice your intent.

2. It isn't likely you will make much progress until the owner is convinced that you have the necessary credentials for giving advice. Perhaps this can come through extra training and continuous application of what you've learned and a lot of perserverance.

3. Introduce new ideas by emphasizing that they will cut costs, reduce stress and take less time. It's always possible that the owner will take credit for your work, but he may rely upon you for planning, when he realizes how much you know.

4. Treat your approach as a challenge. It may become more rewarding than you can imagine.

For authoritarian personalities, the range of choices in business problem solving gets more narrow over time. The scope of business solutions is reduced to those that have worked well in the past.

Continuous Achievement

Continuous achievement breeds confidence, and with it a low tolerance for new and dynamic solutions to business problems. What has worked in the past is the best option for the future. Our mistaken belief is that we've seen it all—from business cycles and personnel practices to material shortages. This, in effect, blocks the family business owner's creativity. In other words, success breeds success, and behavior is solidly reinforced. This makes it almost impossible to step back and see an issue in its entirety.

Gary started a business as a new automobile broker. He provided the best deal in town and had customers from all over. He worked closely with the bank to finance cars for his customers. It was an arrangement that worked nicely for more than 20 years.

When Gary's son Julian graduated from college, he went to work for his dad. They had a respectable agreement as long as Julian didn't try to exercise too much authority. Every time Julian got ready to resolve a problem on his own, his dad would either tell him what to do or take charge of the situation himself. Julian decided that maybe his father was right this time, but eventually he would have the chance to handle things on his own. He knew that no matter how much he tried, he wasn't going to penetrate the veil of his father's authority.

The business did quite well until the economy slumped. Former customers kept their cars longer or bought cheaper models. Gary's father worked closely with the lenders and spent much of his time attending to the company's finances. Julian asked many times to be brought in on some of the meetings with the bank and lenders so that he could learn how the process worked, but Gary kept saying the lenders were his friends—his customers got what they needed.

Julian didn't worry much until he began to see his father's friends at the bank retire or take early leave. He offered to go to the bank officers and try to develop a relationship with some of the younger professionals to preserve continuity. "No," was his father's response. "Don't upset what we have in place!"

This story has a sad ending. Gary thought the frustration of running the company was too much for him. His customers were having a harder time getting loans on good terms and were going elsewhere to purchase their vehicles. Julian wanted to make a purchase deal with his father, but Gary told him, once again, that he didn't know enough to solve these problems and recover their business. So he sold what was left to someone else.

Ignoring Death and Finiteness

Gary and Allen are a perfect examples of business owners who had ample time to resolve succession issues but chose instead to ignore them. When Allen died, the business was divided up among family members who had little interest or understanding of how to manage the business. Luckily for the family, Robert was excited and ready to accept responsibility for his family's predicament.

Finding a Counselor

You may find yourself with questions about the suitability for starting your own business or buying one already in operation. Other professional such as lawyers, accountants, and financial advisors, are typically not comfortable guiding someone through the emotional, psychological and family implications of resolving personal conflicts. Equally important is involving a counselor when the children of a founder find themselves in a situation where they encounter resistance from the parent regarding their personal goals and the status quo.

You Can Do It!!!

Check with friends. They may be helpful in giving feedback about professionals you are considering. Call your trade associations for recommendations. Ask for names of clients served by these professionals. Another avenue to explore is the referral service for your area. Remember that whatever you decide about a consultant or team to work with you, the key is your involvement in all steps.

Summary

This chapter has furnished many examples of the personality characteristics of the successful family business owner. Do some or all of them fit you? This list is not inclusive, but stresses the traits most often observed.

Checklist

❏ Entrepreneurship requires several important personality characteristics:

   a. Expertise

   b. Independence

   c. People evaluation skills

   d. Risk taking

   e. Determination to do the job

❏ Success can reduce our desire to improve.

❏ The counselor's role in family business is to uncover every aspect of an issue. Decisions are not the counselor's to make, however, but the client's.

Personal Considerations Questionnaire: Part I

Y = Yes   **N = No**   **S = Sometimes**

1. Do you like to make your own decisions?	Y	N	S
2. Is implementing your own ideas important to you?	Y	N	S
3. Do you enjoy personal challenges on the job?	Y	N	S
4. Do you like competition in sports, work, etc.?	Y	N	S
5. When you implement your ideas are you usually successful?	Y	N	S
6. Do you get frustrated when things don't go your way?	Y	N	S
7. Do you believe you possess good common sense?	Y	N	S
8. Do you get carried away with your ideas?	Y	N	S
9. Can you work well within time frames?	Y	N	S
10. Is your work not completed until you are satisfied with the product?	Y	N	S
11. Are you willing to work extra hours without extra financial benefit?	Y	N	S
12. Are you willing to stay on the job until it is completed?	Y	N	S
13. Can you live with your job never being finished?	Y	N	S
14. If necessary, are you willing to terminate an employee?	Y	N	S
15. Are you willing to do manual labor if required?	Y	N	S

16. Can you live with being all things to all people?   Y   N   S

17. Do you like being the one who has the final word and takes responsibility for it?   Y   N   S

18. Are you willing to delegate important tasks to someone else?   Y   N   S

19. Are you generally flexible in your work setting and leisure time?   Y   N   S

20. Do you require a great deal of free time for recreation and re-energizing?   Y   N   S

21. Are you willing to risk everything to make a business profitable?   Y   N   S

22. Do you have assets available to pledge for financing?   Y   N   S

23. Is your spouse uncomfortable about what you are planning for your future?   Y   N   S

24. Are you prepared to go back to school to learn new skills?   Y   N   S

25. Are you concerned about your spouse being the sole family support for awhile in order to make your idea work?   Y   N   S

26. Have you thought about asking relatives for money to get this business started?   Y   N   S

27. Do you know what your breakeven point will be?   Y   N   S

28. Are you prepared to be a bill collector if needed?   Y   N   S

29. Are you willing to sign personal guarantees to suppliers and lenders?   Y   N   S

30. Are you worried about whether or not your new company can pay you a livable salary?   Y   N   S

Personal Considerations Questionnaire: Part II

1. *Do you like to make your own decisions?*

No one will tell you if you've made the correct decision. Only the market place and profit and loss statement will validate your decisions.

2. *Do you want the final word and can you take responsibility for it?*

Because no one will decide for you, you must be accountable. At times this might mean rectifying a bad decision.

3. *Are you willing to work long days?*

Owning your own business will require extra hours every day and many weekends. Making the commitment to own a business means you do the work that no one else wants to do and make sure everything is ready for the next day. You must be willing to commit to doing this, not once but many times, without extra compensation.

4. *Are you willing to stay on the job until it is completed?*

If an order needs to be completed for a timely delivery, you have to, at unexpected times, oversee its completion.

5. *Are you willing to do manual labor?*

You may not expect to load and unload trucks. But if necessary, you must be willing to change a tire, load trucks, sweep the floors, etc.

6. *Are you willing to risk everything to achieve profitability?*

Sometimes you must pledge even your home to get needed capital. The risk is great and anything can happen. Will you take that chance?

7. *Is your spouse comfortable with your plan for the future?*

Your partner must be supportive of your move. If not, the trust between you will diminish and may never be recovered. No one expects a smooth path, but a shared risk is much better than going alone.

8. *Will your spouse be the sole support for the family while you develop your ideas?*

This is an expression of your team work. If it won't be possible for you to take a salary for a year or so, someone else can help. Remember to provide for their interests in the new structure.

9. *Are you prepared to become a bill collector if needed?*

In your previous employment, someone else probably did this job. No one really likes collections, but the boss must often take the initiative and make the calls.

ASK YOURSELF

▶ What are the qualities you have that lead you to believe you can survive running a family business?

▶ Why do you want to work for yourself?

▶ What will the effect be on a) your family b) your friends c) your finances?

CHAPTER THREE

TAKING CHARGE ISN'T EASY

HOW TO TAKE CHARGE

Six years before his death, Allen met Wayne at a local lumber-yard. Wayne was a salesman marketing lumber to custom-home builders. Allen was impressed with Wayne's ability to talk to customers. They both had a common hobby in model railroads.

Allen saw the need to expand his operations, particularly the inside administration. He talked to Wayne on several occasions about working in his cabinet shop. He didn't make a serious offer until he learned that the lumberyard was being sold to a local competitor. Allen guessed that Wayne's job was in jeopardy and knew he would be an asset to the expanding team in the cabinet company. Wayne settled on an attractive salary, a truck and general authority to make decisions as needed. When Allen retired in a few years, Wayne felt he could put himself in a position to follow Allen as owner and general manager. Wayne started his new job with great enthusiasm.

Allen and Wayne got along fine as long as things went smoothly. Wayne worked hard and put in long hours to learn the business. After a few months, Allen relinquished new responsibilities to Wayne. There seemed to be mutual respect and Wayne began to take on more administrative directives without any formal assignment by Allen. The first three years passed productively and profitably.

When Allen got sick, Wayne started doing things for Allen that Allen couldn't do for himself. He began to work closely with the estimating staff and set prices without talking it over with Allen. When Allen found out, he was angry. They talked about what to do and decided Wayne should have a greater involvement in pricing, but this fragile agreement came apart when Allen found out that Wayne had attended a creditor's meeting with a big customer and hadn't told him. Allen blew up and called off all prior agreements.

With a little time to think about it, Allen realized what was happening. He saw that Wayne had energetically worked himself into a secure position with the company. Wayne now had most of the customers calling him directly, and the employees turned to him for help and advice.

Allen's brother Jim had been the top salesman of the company long before Wayne was hired. Allen hoped Jim would support his concerns about Wayne and was disappointed when he refused to take a stand on either side of the issue. Although Jim had never shown any interest in managing the company, Allen had always turned to him when he needed someone to talk to about day-to-day frustrations and achievements. Now he felt he had lost Jim's support when he really needed it. Allen was concerned that he was losing control of his company and nobody cared. He told Grace that he couldn't fire Wayne because he would just set up shop across town and take the customers with him. Allen also knew that he was too sick and tired to jump back into the business and rebuild it. Then Allen died during surgery.

At the beginning of this situation, Grace was mostly confused. She wanted to support Allen, but thought Wayne was working in the best interests of the company. After a couple of weeks of Allen's complaints, she too feared that Wayne was merely feathering his own nest. When Allen died, she believed that neither Wayne nor anyone else at the company could be trusted.

Management by a Nonfamily Member

Wayne was helpful to the family when Allen died. He picked up friends and family at the airport, kept the business intact, and his wife did a lot of cooking for Grace the first few weeks after the funeral. Grace was grateful but unsure about what to do with her feelings of distrust. As soon as she could, she discussed these apprehensions with Robert.

Wayne wanted Grace to make business decisions about issues with which she had little familiarity. Allen had never included her on financial decisions and, aside from social contact, she didn't know the suppliers, clients, bankers or accountants. She feared that Wayne would so overwhelm her that she would say "yes" to anything he requested. Although she wanted to keep an interest in the company, she was now afraid to use her power to make decisions that might in some way damage the business. Robert had always been the son who would listen and she needed him now.

Over the next few months, Robert met with Wayne several times and began to understand how his mother felt. Wayne was very independent and already acted like the owner of the company. The discussions seemed circumspect: Wayne was very careful about what he said and how he said it. He got defensive about issues of profitability and employee relationships.

What Robert had hoped for was a friendly, supportive kind of relationship with Wayne. He was willing to support Wayne's attitude of proprietorship with the company if he would just talk openly about the business. He offered to be a buffer between Wayne and his mother in order to keep her from feeling threatened by Wayne's manner.

Meanwhile, Wayne was looking for someone to finance his purchase of Grace's stock. He didn't tell Robert about his interest at first because he wanted to negotiate with Grace exclusively, but when he was turned down for financing a third time, he finally told Robert of his intentions. Robert reacted with surprise, and then caution. To keep Wayne involved, Robert and his mother made an informal agreement with him, including broadening responsibilities in the company.

Entering the Business as a New Family Member

Entering a family business as a new member will require some sensitivity and common sense when it comes to working with existing management and executive employees. They, like everyone else, will be concerned about what it means to have a new family member, inexperienced in the operations of the company and maybe even new to management, enter at the ownership level. They worry about what will be expected of them, how to train the new person and who will be expendable once the training is complete. Invariably, someone at the management level will believe that any intervention in the status quo is an intrusion. Rumors might fly about how the new family member will drain the company profits while everyone else does all the work.

There is a common fear that a new family member manager will give less than their best for the company. Personality differences and questions of authority will emerge. Let them be expressed. The more you know about what each employee wants and needs, the more quickly you can assess your management team. It is in your best interests to give each employee as much latitude during this period as possible so that you may best observe their effectiveness to the company.

Learn quickly the staffing pattern of your family business. Speak with the people critical to the operations of the company. Discuss your plan for the company and their future in it. Make certain they know you will observe and listen for a period of time, then meet with them again to conduct long-range planning.

Don't be too anxious to redefine roles and jobs. After several months, individual meetings with management will enable you to establish how to work with each person. Once these new arrangements are in place, you can monitor their performance. Meanwhile, the business is operating as usual, and you've learned the capabilities of each management person.

Your Turn

Answer this question:

► Do you view resentment by long-term employees as an obstacle in taking over a family business?

► If so, do you feel able to discuss this issue with these workers?

Returning home after a visit to Grace, Robert couldn't put all the business problems out of his mind. He could visibly see the change in his mother. She was trying to remake her life after the death of her husband, and now had her suspicions about Wayne to cope with. In discussions with his wife, Robert became more and more convinced that he should buy his mother's stock and take full control of the company.

Once Robert decided he had what it took to run the business, he started the purchase process, knowing it would take several months before he could assume full-time management. In the meantime, someone from the family needed to be in charge.

Robert enthusiastically accepted this responsibility, knowing that it meant resolving the issue of control with Wayne. "I really wanted a friend to work with," Robert said, "but I don't think that is possible." He continued to talk about how Wayne intimidated him with his knowledge of the business and treated him like a beginning salesman. At the same time, Wayne would ask him to solve a problem that Robert didn't have the background information to resolve: "Just yesterday he called me long distance to make a decision about purchasing health care insurance. He knew I didn't have the financial information to make a good choice, but he kept pressuring me to make the decision that day. Wayne refused to offer his opinion about the most cost-effective and employee-positive option. He just stated that if I was to be in charge, I would have to make the decision." Robert was angry.

Wayne was testing Robert's authority, knowledge and ability to make management decisions. He was undermining Robert until Robert could figure out how to assert control. Susan had encountered some of the same frustrations Robert was feeling.

Employee Resentment

Susan's father owned a computer products and service store. After his second heart attack, the doctor mandated surgery and some time off from the stress of business. Susan wasn't a permanent employee of the store, but she spent time there while she was in college helping out at night and on weekends. Her father was relieved that Susan was willing to manage the store in his absence. She was familiar with her father's management style and operation of the store, but knew that computers and their related technology changed so frequently she would need to rely heavily on the technical staff.

She called a brief meeting her first morning on the job and explained that she wanted everything to be "business as usual." Susan got her first clue that this wasn't going to be easy when the top salesman blurted out that a planned delivery hadn't arrived and the customer was furious. Susan spent several hours on the phone trying to follow up, appease the customer and figure out what to do. Then it occurred to her that the salesman had been employed by the store before her dad bought the business. Surely he knew what was policy in these circumstances. In consultation with him she discovered that they usually sent out the display model until the ordered one came in. "Why didn't you say that hours ago?" she asked. "Well," the salesman stated, "your dad always handled problems by himself and you said to do everything just like before."

After settling the problem with the delivery, Susan met again with the staff. She declared that she was not there to solve problems they already knew how to handle. "Let me know about the situation, but come ready to resolve it yourself. You are the experts and can do a good job in making responsible decisions," Susan explained. "I'm going to tell my father that your expertise can save him a lot of stress on the job, so he can put his energy into problems only the owner needs to handle."

Require Daily Reports and Keep a Log

Telling Robert about Susan's technique gave Robert an idea of how to work with Wayne, especially during this transition period. "I don't want to alienate him," he said. "What do you think about a regular meeting so that he can update me on the week's activities and upcoming work? During that time he can give me recommendations about what to do, until I can be in the office on a daily basis."

"Sounds fine to me," I said, "but how will you prevent getting steamrolled by him? Why not set up a telephone schedule so that he must report to you daily?"

"I'll have to try it for a while," Robert declared. "At least he'll know I'm in charge, even though he's managing the company on a day-to-day basis."

"The only thing I might add," I suggested, "is that you keep a detailed log about your meetings so you can refer to your decisions and plans."

Making the Transition from Employee to Employer

After years of reporting to someone else, the thought of having autonomy to make all important business decisions seems very attractive. It doesn't take long, however, to realize that without someone else to make decisions and give directions, the role of owner isn't as easy as it seems. The successful transition from employee to owner can only be accomplished with a great deal of thought and planning.

Few employees see the broad range of issues an owner must handle. Decision making at the top requires a great deal of faith and fortitude. The willingness to work long hours and gamble all your resources are prerequisites to owning your own business. Learning to take responsibility for the actions of people you hire can be a dramatic realization. No one will evaluate your job performance. Only a profit-and-loss statement will validate your business philosophy and practices. There will be no one to turn to for guidance. The acid test of your initiative will be your success in the marketplace. Handling people, customers, employees and family members will take on a new dimension and they all are important to your success.

Take your time to make the decision to commit yourself to a family business venture. Spend time if you can with other owner-managers in your field, learn what it will take financially, what kinds of personal changes you will experience and what may be required of your family to enable you to succeed.

Answer the following:

► Have you spoken to a lawyer about the responsibilities and liabilities of owning a business? What did you learn?

► Have you spoken to an accountant about the costs of doing business and the necessity of monitoring those costs? Do you feel capable of managing these expenses?

► Have you investigated the market conditions and other aspects of the business? What are your hesitations? Where might you search for more information and assistance?

Developing Competence in the Field

While feeling more comfortable because he was asserting his position with Wayne, Robert was still concerned about Wayne's decision making. "Not only do I have to learn how to make the big decisions in areas like finances, staffing and leadership," Robert declared, "I also have to learn how to sell our product. Dad showed me the difference long ago between quality construction and adequate work, but I never thought I would have to employ the knowledge. This is a skill I certainly didn't need as a banker. Is there any way I can get over my apprehension about exposing my incompetence in estimating, scheduling or salesmanship?"

Learning a new business is hard for everyone. We all make many mistakes, but the key is to turn them into positive experiences. I said, "Think back to when you started with the bank. Slowly but surely you learned to feel confident that you could handle any situation. This experience will be similar, except you will be the boss. You don't have someone to explain how it all works, but remember that your employees are experts who know all phases of the business. Use them. They will feel flattered that you consider them competent and you will learn along the way."

I told Robert that I was once just where he is, and my rush to know everything got me in trouble. When my father died he left a thriving, profitable commercial and residential insulation business to my mother. After a few months, I made an arrangement with her to enter the business and learn from the general manager. My intent was to work in the company just long enough to make it self-sustaining for my mother and sister, who were dependent on the company for their living.

Helping around the shop as a kid does not teach you how the business really works. I started my education by learning how to do an estimate. After mastering the rudiments, I went out into the marketplace to try out my new estimating skills. The first few jobs I calculated were with contractors who were friends of the family. They were patient and signed my contracts right away. After some experience at this, I began to feel more and more confident. Then I got a call from a builder about 85 miles from town. I wanted to look at the job because the architect-builder said it was an interesting design. He was right. The house was unlike anything I had ever seen. I went about doing my measurements, asked questions and finally produced my estimate. The builder was impressed with my price and signed my contract right away. That should have been my first warning.

We scheduled the job for a few days later. As our work progressed, I conducted a cost analysis to see how well I'd estimated the job. You can imagine my surprise when I learned the company had lost $600 on this job. I had totally mismeasured and miscalculated the whole house. I felt terribly incompetent. It took me a long time before I'd estimate another job that was out of the ordinary.

It helps to know that even those who seem the most competent started out learning the hard way. The struggles you encounter in learning will have a cumulative effect. Your experience will be valuable in future problem solving.

When a Relative in Your Employment Poses a Problem

Relatives on the payroll require a different response from you than anyone else when they exhibit personal problems. Drug abuse, alcohol addiction or emotional problems demand consideration for the person as well as the company and family members. If an unrelated employee has personal problems affecting their job performance, your range of alternatives is usually guided by past resolution and company policy. However, in the case of a relative who works for you, a lifetime of family experiences and feelings must be considered.

Your response to the person experiencing problems is important in gaining the confidence of everyone involved, including family members and other employees.

Steps to Take with a Problem Employee

The following steps will help you manage the potentially emotional situation.

1. Determine how the problem relative materially affects your business or interferes with your customers, associates and family.

2. Meet with other employees to determine the full spectrum of the problem.

3. Notify the relative that you are aware of a problem and reach agreement with them about what to do.

4. If the relative is uncooperative, tell your employee's closest family member that you intend to intervene.

5. If the behavior is not remedied, bring in a professional to assist in intervention. Follow the directions of the professional.

6. Record your impressions of the interaction and determine if employment must be terminated. Outline your policy for if and when the relative returns to work.

It's possible that the intervention will bring about an emotional response, and the relative at first may want to leave rather than receive professional help to solve a personal problem. Ask the relative to reconsider and seek treatment. Maintaining a sense of personal dignity is important to anyone going through a tough and emotional time, but if you reach a point where you are spending more time with this situation than it warrants, make a settlement that you can live with and terminate the relative.

You Can Do It!!!

Make information available about community resources for drug abuse, alcohol addiction and counseling centers. This may be part of your medical or employee handbook information given to all employees. Don't wait for the situation to resolve itself. Helping a relative or other employee can not only change their behavior, but ensure that you retain a valuable, trained employee. Review your plan with other employees for feedback and refinement. Sometimes the best resource is someone who has solved this problem before.

Alcohol Abuse and Intervention

Robert had one more concern that needed to be resolved. Once he stated his interest in managing the company, everyone wanted to talk about Jim. Even Wayne wasn't willing to make suggestions about the salesman. He wanted to have the family intervene in this business problem.

Jim's problems had been with him for a long time, but they are more acute now than ever. Although the family had always been willing to laugh off his drinking because he's such a great guy, he's becoming a danger to himself, company employees and property. Several employees, Wayne and Grace asked Robert to do something about him before he hurt himself further.

Jim was the oldest son in the family. He had a personality that made his siblings and friends admire him. Grandma thought he was terrific and helped him out of any trouble spots. His athletic ability made him the local star, always the toast of the bar. He got accustomed to free drinks, local celebrity status and life in the easy lane.

Jim loved everybody and everybody loved him. He moved from business to business and marriage to marriage never taking responsibility for his life. He never wanted children of his own, but he loved his nieces and nephews. Robert grew up thinking his uncle's style of living was exciting. He always told great stories, laughing about how his problems were always someone else's fault. Allen and Grace knew that Jim's lack of ambition was due to his drinking. Jim had tried several times to change, but never managed to stay dry for long.

Finally, he met a great woman who helped him stay sober. Jim convinced Allen that he was a changed man, and Allen agreed to try him out in the cabinet business. Jim was a born salesman. When he was hired, business was at its peak. The job was perfect for his outgoing personality, so Jim thrived. He was finally ready to settle down. He and his wife bought a house. However, part of his job as a salesman required Jim to entertain socially—where he once again made choices about his drinking. He became a very careful drunk, convincing himself that he could deceive his wife, Allen and customers.

When his wife realized what was happening, she became frightened. She took this change personally and sought refuge in her job. She also began to attend Alcoholics Anonymous meetings and left AA literature around the house for Jim to read. But Jim was entrenched in drinking.

When Allen told Jim about his cancer, Jim tried to keep his drinking under control, and it worked for a while. But as Allen got sicker, Jim's problems became more apparent. Allen didn't confront Jim because he had enough to handle. He knew Jim was drinking but told no one, not even Grace.

Grace found it difficult to respect Jim. They had been close, but she tried not to interfere with his working relationship with Allen. Her boys loved their uncle—he was the one who taught them sports. His athletic skills had been a magnet. Jim took them fishing, camping or to football games. They never forgot this influence on them, especially Robert.

However, the rest of the company was keenly aware that Jim was drunk most of the time. They covered for him because they didn't want to upset Allen. They knew Jim couldn't help recover lost business, and he often added to the problems by forgetfulness and lack of attention to detail. Wayne knew that Allen relied on his brother to listen to his day. If Wayne tried to remove Jim, Allen would see this as proof of Wayne's desire to control the company. Wayne waited out the problem, hoping he might someday buy the business.

Jim's drinking accelerated after his brother's death. His wife felt helpless to talk him into sobriety. Grace just didn't want him around, and the other employees were tired of covering for his incompetence. When Jim damaged a company truck pulling out of his favorite after-work drinking spot, the insurance company refused to cover him. It was not his first accident, and everyone knew it wouldn't be his last. Now "what to do about Jim" had become Robert's problem.

Robert knew everyone in the company was watching how he handled his uncle. He didn't want to offend Jim, but he had to act in the best interest of the company. Jim's behavior hurt a lot of people and endangered employees' welfare, but Robert feared that his uncle would probably just laugh at him.

In discussing the issue Robert drew on his experiences at the bank. He remembered that the insurance carrier for the bank provided counseling for people with alcohol and drug addictions, including a provision for hospitalization for detoxification. He recalled how much this had helped a fellow he knew in the trust department. Robert thought he might start researching treatment alternatives. Although Alcoholics Anonymous was an option, he knew Jim needed something pretty dramatic to get him past his chemical dependency. There didn't seem to be any other option than to go through the medical plan, even though it might result in a rate hike for the company. He was planning to formulate a plan within the next few days.

Robert wasn't at all sure how he would get Jim to cooperate without alienating him. I assured him that the end result was to get his uncle the help he needed. He could worry about his family relationship to Jim later.

Family Interventions Are Best

Talking to his uncle alone worried Robert. His major fear was that Uncle Jim would feel Robert was looking out for the company only. Robert thought he could get his mother, sister and Jim's wife to be in the room with him when he talked to his uncle. If successful, they would then go to the hospital or counseling center directly and get started on a prearranged treatment plan. Robert decided that if his uncle would not cooperate, he would ask him to resign. Robert was prepared to offer a liberal termination settlement, but hoped he wouldn't need to use this option. As part of the plan, Robert wanted to hold his uncle's job for three months with a review of his progress. This was flexible and could be changed at any time. Once Robert's plan was firm, he discussed it with Wayne to get his feedback and support.

The day after the meeting Robert called me to report that it went as well as could be expected. At first his uncle had been angry and resentful, but then resigned himself to going to the hospital. Robert was relieved and looked forward to a good night's sleep.

A Successful Intervention

Robert had done all he could to assist his uncle and, in turn, reassure his family and employees that he was in control. Instead of losing his uncle's respect, he had gained stature as a decision maker. "You definitely are your father's son," Wayne commented.

He realized that his education in decision making was just beginning. He felt much more confident now. While Wayne would never be his confidant, he knew they could now work together toward a common goal. Roles had been established that would be easy to maintain once Robert took over day-to-day management. Robert had a lot to learn, but instead of feeling overwhelmed, he could take his time finding out what staff and business resources were available to him.

Family Business Conflict Situations

SITUATION

Your second in command (an employee of 12 years) has just informed you that while you were away on a week's vacation, a long-term employee was seriously injured in an accident. After you get the details, your reaction turns to anger. Why hadn't the manager called to inform you?

PROPOSED RESOLUTION

The owner needs to take steps to prevent this situation from happening again. It would be useful to meet with the assistant and reiterate what is expected in these situations. It's possible that a conference may be enough to reach an understanding about your need to be informed in the future. If you believe there are problems in your relationship with the second in command, now may be a good time to record the meeting and ask that a written documentation be signed by the employee.

SITUATION

You've recently hired a new sales manager. He's young, aggressive, successful and a computer fanatic. The first few months have been very productive, but lately you've noticed him staying in the office longer and longer each day. You learn that he has been computerizing all the sales district boundaries and is about to reassign new districts to the sales force. You know that some long-term employees will be hurt. When you sit down with him to ask about his reason for doing this, he gets defensive. He finishes with a self-serving diatribe about being the only progressive and forward-looking person in the company. He says you should leave him alone to do the job you hired him for. How would you go about diffusing this situation?

PROPOSED RESOLUTION

It's possible that this energetic sales manager is carrying out what he considers to be his mission with the company. If he feels he has authority to redesign the sales territories and reassign salespeople, any other message will be a surprise to him. This could be the time to re-establish goals and direction. If the owner is concerned about the changes the new manager is making, a longer meeting with him might help to clear up misinformation and lay the groundwork for new policy.

SITUATION

You've had some really bad luck the past few years. Last year you sent your accountant to an alcohol-treatment facility. After a month, he returned to work. Three months later he announced he was going to change careers and quit. The month-long stay in the treatment center cost your insurance company $20,000, and you paid the accountant's salary during his absence. This spring your top salesperson went to a facility to get treatment for cocaine abuse. Although he is back on the job, he can't seem to stay focused on his tasks. What can you do to prevent these situations from occurring again?

PROPOSED RESOLUTION

The business environment today addresses a much greater range of employees' personal problems than ever before. Alcohol addiction and drug problems can be controlled only by the user. If an employee needs hospitalization and possibly long-term care, the employer should research available and affordable treatment plans. This would enable both of them to work together for optimal recovery. Even with the best treatment center, it isn't always possible for some people to adjust to abstinence in a short time. Only with continuous treatment can there be a good chance for recovery and normalization at the work place.

4.

SITUATION

You own a small telephone equipment company and have been in business for five years. During that time your secretary has been a capable and loyal employee. The past few months you've observed some erratic behavior from her. One day she's emotionally high and two days later is hostile or in the dumps. You've become worried because her performance at work has begun to change. One day you ask what is wrong and she snaps at you to leave her alone. You don't want to fire her, but if you knew what to do, you'd do it. What is your next step in this situation?

PROPOSED RESOLUTION

Recognizing the difference between personality traits and mental health problems can be difficult. One way to gauge whether or not you've encountered mental illness is to recognize your reaction and feelings to the situation. If something so troubles you that you are extremely uncomfortable, you may need to seek professional advice. It would be useful to have at your desk a community resource guide listing support services available in your area. If an employee resists assistance, be firm and urge response at some point within the near future. If the reticence continues, then it might be best to make seeking help a condition of employment. This is appropriate only after all other strategies have been exhausted.

ASK YOURSELF

▶ Are there key employees in the company who need special attention and consideration? Define these conditions and how you will handle them.

▶ Discuss how you will handle the inevitable conflicts and misunderstandings that will arise during the ownership transition period.

▶ How will you identify the employees in the company who will give you the information you need to operate the business?

▶ If you need to hire new key personnel from the outside, describe your plans to integrate the outsiders.

CHAPTER FOUR

COMMUNICATION, COOPERATION AND CONTROL

THE KEYS TO SUCCESS

It didn't take long for Robert to move from being a minority stockholder to full-time manager of the family business. He and Rachel sold their home, terminated their jobs and settled into a new and exciting challenge. The sale of his mother's stock was quickly completed and Robert was ready to become a family business owner.

In a follow-up session, Robert remarked that he sensed that resolving personnel issues would be a large part of his day-to-day business. Although he was happy that he had come up with solutions to the issues with Wayne and his Uncle Jim,

he thought he needed more training and preparation in personnel management.

Robert felt secure only about his management functions of planning, customer relations and financial matters. As a midlevel manager with the bank, Robert had little exposure to matters he was now expected to face. His foremost concern was the unresolved issues between his mother, siblings and himself.

"What can I do to keep everyone off my back while I learn this business?" Robert asked. "My mother wants this, my sister wants that and my brother wants something else. I thought my agreements with them were going to provide me the time I needed to gain control of this business."

Gaining Support for Your Policies

There are essential ingredients in gaining support from family and employees. These "three C's" are communication, cooperation and control.

► Communication

Decide early on whether you want relatives, children or a spouse to receive financial or operations reports about the company. Be advised, however, that once you've started to inform them about the operations of the company, it will be difficult to exclude them at a later time. When family members have needed background and current information, they can more easily provide support when needed. This is an effective way to avoid conflict about the status of the business.

Communication can be accomplished via newsletters, quarterly financial reports and annual meetings. Other meetings may be scheduled as needed to gather input about major company decisions.

► Cooperation

Regular and thorough communication will go a long way toward garnering support from the family about major decisions. Treating family as administrative resources, rather then potential adversaries, will assist in the results you desire. It is not necessary for someone to be a professional in your field to give good suggestions.

Cooperation is the by-product of good communication. Listen to suggestions and solicit information regularly. Your relatives and employees will give you extra effort and commitment when they have a stake in the outcome of your decisions.

► Control

Control of your family business means you have accepted accountability for your decisions and the actions of your employees. To have full authority without provoking resentment in the company, you must use it judicially. You should have no problem with control if your actions are responsible and tactful.

Your Turn   *Answer the following:*

► Do you have a plan to communicate information about the business?

► List five types of information you plan to include in family updates.

► Who will you assign responsibility for gathering and distributing this information?

Summarizing the Three C's

We talked about the three C's in family business: communication, cooperation and control. Don't leave family members in the dark about what you are doing and how it affects them. An owner must think about ways to communicate with family so that all information about the company is made available to them. This enables the owner to maintain day-to-day control.

You Can Do It!!!

Gather the family together and solicit their ideas about an information-sharing scheme. Assign someone to develop necessary information for family communication, such as a newsletter, reporting format or financial statements. Establish regular meetings where you can report on business progress. Make sure your information sharing includes your company *vision, policies* and *accountability.* Think about establishing a *board of directors,* including several family members, so that the family could be involved in policy making.

Surviving a Spouse

Family businesses are complex organizations that need a lot of special attention, unlike a lot of other enterprises. In Robert's case, even though he purchased Grace's share of the business, she still has an interest in what he does. She has lived with this company through Allen for many years. Her daily routine is probably still oriented around him and his management practices. For years, she was dependent upon him for income, security and companionship. She's not going to change much very soon. It's not surprising that she wants a greater role in the business and Robert's affairs. Maybe she wants to make sure that Robert extends to her all the benefits of the business she used to enjoy.

EXAMPLE

Many spouses of entrepreneurs feel dispossessed when their loved one dies. Lillian's husband was a cleaning supply wholesaler. She often worked in the business during busy periods or when the assistant or bookkeeper took vacations. She didn't mind going to work when needed, and it helped her understand her husband's day. It gave her an appreciation for his problems and an insight into his moods.

Over the years, the supply business provided them with nice vacations, a comfortable home and a good education for their children. Ron, the youngest, worked for his father as a salesman. It was planned that at some time he would take over the company, but when Bill died suddenly, he left no instructions for who was to manage in his absence. Although Lillian inherited the company stock, she had no idea what to do with it. She approached Ron about running the business. He agreed and began to put together a management team that would work for him. The challenge was so absorbing that he neglected to tell his mother about the changes he was making.

When Lillian realized that Ron was using the business for some personal luxuries (leased car, supplier entertainment) in making his industry connections, she began to worry about her status. She asked him what he was doing—and wasn't satisfied with Ron's explanation. He didn't think his mother had reason to question his practices because she was receiving plenty of money and the company was profitable. He told his mother that if she interfered, it would create a lot of internal confusion that would just add to her frustration and concern.

Lillian decided to accept her son's reasoning, but she felt uncomfortable about what was going on. She wasn't happy that all the luxuries were going to her son while none of her other children were benefiting from the business. She kept her feelings on the shelf until one day she learned that Ron had purchased a rather expensive boat, through the company, and had it delivered to the lake, without telling her what he had done.

This act pushed Lillian to call Ron and demand a meeting. He showed up indignant. Lillian was so mad she told Ron he no longer had the authority to take advantage of the company. "If you don't come up with some kind of plan to institute checks and balances, I'm going to sell the business out from under you," she said.

Ron, of course, was surprised, but knew his mother meant everything she said. He made the boat available to the family, immediately instituted regular meetings with his mother and produced a monthly newsletter for everyone in the family. His most inspired plan was to assemble a board of directors, which included many family members.

Lillian now felt secure about what Ron was doing. This was the kind of role she had hoped for. She didn't like the watchdog role and felt more comfortable with a broad range of professionals and family members overseeing the business. Now she felt she could relax and enjoy the fruits of her husband's hard work.

Communication

Now that the three C's have been introduced, let's explore each of them in detail. Each of these three major elements is important to maintain good relations in the family business. Each factor dependents on the other.

In a family business, one of the most positive relationship builders is regular and meaningful communication. When all interested parties are brought up to date on policy, decision making and planning—and have some input in its formulation—everyone has a stake in the business's success and commitment to follow through.

Children may feel disenfranchised from the family enterprise. Not all children need to have a say about the business, but in instances where a principal passes away and children benefit from the estate, there seems to be good reason to have them involved in its future.

Family members don't like to talk about trust in financial matters, but it is an important element. If trust is not established early, it is difficult to bring it about later. It's not uncommon for each family member to hire an attorney to represent their own interests. The outcome of this is never good. Optimism and family feelings go out the window. When bitterness is introduced, too often things are said and actions taken that can never be resolved.

EXAMPLE

Don was involved in his father's new car dealership. He had two sisters: one worked in the accounting department, and the other, Lisa, lived out of state. Lisa had been resentful for some time about her brother and sister working for her father. Her father had explained many times that her sister and brother worked hard for their salary and benefits. If she wanted to partake, she could work as hard as they did.

When their father died, he left one half of the business to his wife and equal shares of his estate, including the company, to his children. Lisa felt she had a right to demand as much from the company as her brother and sister were getting in salary, profit sharing and other benefits while maintaining her shares in the company. One last time her mother and siblings tried to explain to Lisa that they would not give her money unless she contributed time and resources like the others. She would have to be satisfied with a share of the profits.

Lisa saw a lawyer, filed suit and challenged the family to see things her way. Eventually she settled for monthly payments, a share of the profits and a complete separation from her family. The feelings on this issue ran so deep that when her mother died Lisa didn't attend the service and sent the lawyer to represent her at the reading of her mother's will.

Lisa wasn't mentioned in the will and her attorney was prepared to file a challenge. After much costly maneuvering, she chose to drop the suit and withdraw. However, no one in the family saw this as a peace offering—nor found reason to continue communication with her.

Whether or not Lisa might have been less angry if some of the family members had brought her into company business planning and decision making won't be known. It is possible that if she'd had a say in events, even at a distance, she might have been more cooperative.

Eric and Maureen were married about eight years ago. At that time, by previous marriages, each had two children ranging from eight to 16. Eric owned six restaurant/taverns in town, and Maureen had been a stockbroker and investment counselor. They decided before they got married that she would stay home and raise the children.

This seemed to be a very satisfactory and successful arrangement for a long time. When the youngest child was 16, Maureen was ready to resume her career outside the home. Eric was happy about the way his family and business had prospered. Only when Maureen told him about her desire to return to work did he perceive what a change like this would mean for all of them.

Eric wasn't prepared for this. He didn't want to think about the consequences of Maureen's fulltime employment. He was afraid of taking more responsibility around the home, but knew she would expect him to participate to a much greater extent. He figured if he was creative enough, he could talk her out of changing the status quo.

Eric felt that his interests and Maureen's could best be served if she were to become involved in the existing business. They decided that Maureen would conduct a financial audit of the firm. This would give her first-hand knowledge of the status of the company. Then, once she had command of the information, she would become the financial investment consultant to the business. This appealed to Maureen because it was an extension of her professional skills, and she could gain access to company financial knowledge that would put her in a well-prepared position if anything happened to Eric.

In addition, Eric was convinced that this would be a good time to inform all the children about the status of the family business. He and Maureen devised a monthly newsletter, which went to all the employees—with a personalized addition to each of their children—including a report on the financial condition of the company and plans for the future. Then they called a family dinner to discuss the direction and management of the company.

Cooperation

Cooperation may not be everything in a relationship or a family business, but without it, success can't be expected. Robert needed to find a way to bring his family around to his approach to business. The only way was to show what he could do by example.

His goal was to gain cooperation with the family by communicating with them about everything important to the functioning of the business. The outcome would be informed feedback to him. Robert developed a set of strategies to get his mother, sister and brother to become active participants in the planning process.

Reporting Strategies

1. Schedule regular status meetings to include any family members interested in attending. These could be announced two weeks in advance. Meetings would cover business for the previous month with projections to the end of the month. Participants could offer any advice they wanted. Where practical, the owner-manager would incorporate any suggestions into day-to-day operations.

2. Establish a newsletter to give all family members and employees a brief overview of activities within the company. Everything from sales information to baby announcements can be included. A suggestion box would be set up for employees to contribute to the monthly publication.

3. Establish a board of directors to include family, employees, an accountant and lawyer. This group is to oversee the company as it works toward short and long-range goals. The board would also establish financial guidelines to give an acting principal the authority to make major purchases. Minutes should be complied of each meeting and distributed to all members of the board.

4. Plan a family reunion once a year to combine work and pleasure. Any interested family member could attend the meeting, at which time the business year would be presented in review. No policy or decision making should be expected at this gathering. The company would pay for as much of the meeting as was allowed by the board.

Start with the Small Issues

Robert concluded that the only way he would get what he wanted was to find ways to get everyone in the immediate family to cooperate. Ingenuity and hard work enabled him to get everyone behind his ideas. He felt that if the family were committed to this course of action, he would have support for the big issues, such as business expansion, capital expenditures for equipment and increased product lines. He also was sure that the company would benefit from examining areas of diversification, which would help it ride out the cycles in the construction business.

It is easy to see how cooperation relates to communication. Robert's approach was to provide information to everyone in the family; then when it came time to make decisions, he would be able to make a case for his ideas because all the issues would be understood. He also knew he couldn't expect universal agreement on all issues. Robert was ready for disagreements and would accept decisions by the majority, but he made it clear to all family members that he wouldn't take unfounded criticism.

Increasing Feeling of Involvement

Robert's ideas were sound and certain to succeed. He put out enough incentives to everyone to get them to cooperate. If he could deliver on his promise of involvement with a payoff in profits—however modest—there seemed no reason for him to fail. We talked about a few more important ideas needed for successful cooperation within a family owned business.

► People need to feel they can *contribute* to the success of the enterprise. Even if it is only to help coordinate the yearly picnic, people need to know their contributions are meaningful.

► Next, participants must feel *competent* at what they do. It makes no sense to ask employees to do a job at which they will fail. To request that someone, for example, prepare a financial report for the group, while not having expertise or knowledge, will court disaster. Next time the person will be hesitant to help with any job outside current tasks. When employees don't get a feeling of success or satisfaction, they will sooner or later try to get out of any involvement at all.

► If an employee feels a sense of *cooperation* with others in similar tasks, then you can reasonably expect good results. Few of us do anything without the help of someone else. Ours is no longer a society of individuals. We need to rely on the good faith and willingness of others to accomplish anything.

► One must feel a sense of *belonging* in an organization, be it family, school, workplace or recreational sports. With a feeling of belonging comes the confidence to try new behaviors, approaches and ideas. In essence, it is the support group that enables a person to feel comfortable being themselves.

If these goals can be fulfilled, the endeavor stands a greater chance for success. To achieve the desired outcome, we need to learn these basic principles for ourselves and others. We must be vigilant about how others think and do things, which will assure that they contribute. Coworkers are competent and will be cooperative in achieving the company's goals.

Control

While Robert had done a great deal for the family and their interests, he was concerned about overall control of the business. He thought that once the communication scheme and cooperative commitment were established, he was now merely a "caretaker" for the family business and without the range of authority he expected.

Robert's concerns were two dimensions of control: *financial* and *leadership.* Financial control had allowed Robert's father to exercise a high level of authority in his business and the marketplace. It allowed him to do whatever he wanted in the company—from paying better wages than the prevailing rate to regulating bidding practices. To secure work, he could adjust the terms of customer payment and pricing, essentially deciding who could pay late and who must pay on time.

Allen was arrogant with his competition. He would take a large certificate of deposit to monthly trade meetings, prop it up in front of his plate and wait for someone to ask him what it was. Then he'd pass it out to them and wait for their reaction. Not everyone was amused. He would strategically underbid all other cabinet makers in the region, knowing he wouldn't make a profit on those jobs, but making his competition wonder what he was up to. Sooner or later this approach would force his competition to decide it wasn't in their best interests to stay in the market.

Robert didn't have the experience of building the business nor the freedom to do always what he wanted. To succeed in the company, he will have to exercise leadership, operate at a level of authority and defend his actions. His father didn't have to do this. Allen answered to no one. Employees did what they were told or moved on. This won't happen with Robert who will have to prove that he knows what he is doing and work to preserve the company for the benefit of all involved.

Leadership Through Integrity

Robert understood that he had to have good, acceptable reasons for everything he did. If he didn't, the board of directors and his family would reject his proposals and prevent him from exercising the range of authority he needed.

Robert also understood that in his position as leader he wouldn't be able to share the blame for his mistakes. He will gain authority and control by demonstrating integrity and trustworthiness. Leadership isn't easy. Of all the situations to put yourself in, this is the most complicated. Not only do the company employees depend on Robert for their livelihood, but now his family expects the same commitment.

Richard and George had run a mining supply company for more than 25 years. Richard was the oldest of the brothers and generally ran the business with George's help. He did most of the administration, ordering of materials, hiring and firing and financial management. George was content to make sales calls and trouble shoot problems. Theirs was a good combination of personality and talent. The business grew substantially until one day George died of a heart attack.

There had been no formal agreement between them about what would happen to each other's share of the company in case one of them died. George had been divorced for some time and had only his son, Ernie, to whom he could leave his estate. Ernie was between jobs as a well rigger and decided to take over his father's half share of the business. Richard was unsure about what might happen because he was now in the position of doing his brother's job as well as his own.

"Why don't you teach me the business," Ernie said, "and I'll buy your share when you want to retire." This seemed like a reasonable proposition to Richard as long as Ernie settled down and really got involved in the company. From the beginning it was a mismatch of personalities.

Ernie was conscientious. He saw opportunities in the marketplace and wanted to take advantage of them. "Why don't we expand our sales into the next state," he said. "I know some people who would buy from us. All it would take is a little more effort and we could establish a new profit base."

"No," said Richard. "It's too far to drive back and forth in a day."

This rejection, however, didn't dissuade Ernie from coming up with other ideas. Each one was treated just like the first. Richard's standard remark was "wait until the company is yours before you jeopardize its success."

After two years of this, Ernie asked Richard to buy out his interest. Richard was astonished that Ernie might want to do such a thing. He reminded him of much money they were making. "Isn't that enough?" he said.

"It's fine," said Ernie, "but I can't wait for you to move on before I can implement some of my new ideas. I've decided to go back to the oil well industry. Within certain limits I can do what I want because I have a good reputation in that field."

Too much control with no give and take will wither enthusiasm and creativity. Richard sold out to a competitor several years later, never changing his controlling personality.

Family Business Conflict Situations

SITUATION

Joanne and Eileen were the only children of Mark and Louise. The daughters lived in different states. When Mark retired he put his daughters on the board of directors of his Big M tire company. His purpose was to keep them informed about the business. Several times a year he had to send them documents for their signature. It has been a problem getting the daughters to return the signed papers, and the problem was getting worse. Their explanation for the delay wasn't too convincing. Mark doesn't want to remove them from the board. How can Mark get better cooperation from his daughters?

PROPOSED RESOLUTION

Mark had a great idea when he put his daughters on the board of directors. It seems, though, that they have other interests and priorities in their lives. Maybe the fee is too small to keep their attention, maybe they don't want to participate in something they feel only remotely concerned about. It would be a good idea for Mark to contact each daughter and discuss what it is he expects. If they understand the importance of the signed documents they may be more willing to return them as needed. He should also try to learn from them whether they really want to be an active member of the board. If they don't, he could redirect his efforts in their behalf.

SITUATION

Your sister owns stock in the family furniture company. She has had little to say about how you manage the store as long as she receives a dividend. However, her husband looks over the financial information his wife receives every quarter. You obviously are making money and he wants more. He has just asked for a breakdown of administrative expenses. What do you think he wants to do with this information? What can you do?

PROPOSED RESOLUTION

This issue can be one of the most divisive of all family business problems. Even though a family member receives a distribution from stock ownership, sometimes this isn't enough for them. Once a dividend payment becomes routine, it is difficult to stop. A stock-holder has a right to information about the business, and family members, especially, feel that it should be available to them. In this case, the manager would do best if a meeting were called to review company progress. At that time, a breakdown of how dividends are paid should be presented. Every detail about the company's financial resources could be reviewed. If there is a continuing request for additional payment without justification, then the matter should be placed on the agenda for the next board meeting. Rely on the board to resolve this problem.

SITUATION

You've been managing your mother's dress shop for the past year since she retired. She has come in on an irregular basis to see how you are doing. As the owner, she depends on the store for her income, but she hasn't adjusted too well to retirement. Lately her attitude toward you has been negative. She complains about your stock, level of inventory and sales tactics. Everything you are doing she claims she can do better. She wants to take you to lunch tomorrow to discuss your management of the store. How do you prepare for this meeting?

PROPOSED RESOLUTION

Moving from career to retirement is never an easy transition. The stimulation of problem solving, planning for contingencies and projecting for the future make it difficult to step aside. On the other hand, when ownership of the store is in the hands of the retiree, there really isn't much you, as a manager, can say. There are a few alternatives that might work. Instead of a management agreement, why not structure a buyout and put the decision making in the hands of the person closest to the business? If the mother will not accept any offer advanced, then the daughter must request a clarification of roles. This should be something they can both live with and be able to maintain. If the mother continues to resist the daughter's management, the daughter should look for other employment opportunities.

ASK YOURSELF

▶ Describe any lines of communication you have established:

- With family members
- By regular reporting

▶ Discuss the assurances you have from your family that they agree to your control of the company and that they will cooperate with your decisions.

CHAPTER
FIVE

INHERITING

A

BUSINESS

WHAT HAPPENS WHEN THE FOUNDER DIES

If you are the relative who emerges as the leader in the family's decision to continue the business, it won't take long to realize that taking control in a time of crisis involves a lot of tension. Issues commonly focus on both the financial preservation of the company and emotion well-being of family members. The family or business' accountants and lawyers will act immediately following the owner's death to detail what actions are needed for business continuity.

Even if a well-developed plan for the continuation of the company has been developed, confusion in the family will likely prevail for some time. This is a critical period when the spouse and children want to know what to expect regarding their interests. The spouse in most cases wants to be assured of financial stability and continued role in the business operation. Adult children want to know if they will have financial responsibility for a parent's welfare. Relatives in the business need to know if they will remain with the company. The anxiety level of everyone is high and a clear statement of what is to happen brings their apprehension under control.

The resolution of major financial issues will have a calming effect for a short time, but pretty soon the long-term issues inherent in family situations, such as personal relationships, sibling rivalries and control, begin to take shape. These emotional issues will need your immediate attention. Often the bickering, hurt feelings, insecurities and anger will be impossible to overcome later on. And they can do irreversible damage to a business at a time when competitors and customers are focusing on the weaknesses of the company.

Be sure to discuss all the issues, including financial, legal, personal and family concerns. You should strive to get the most comprehensive, detailed information possible. You will need it to make decisions about your involvement with the business.

You Can Do It!!!

If you don't have a personal attorney or accountant already familiar with the family business, make appointments for a consultation. The business most likely retains several professionals; but they may or may not be your best resources when making a decision. Remember, they have the best interests of the company in mind, but they may not be the most sound advisors *to you* as a family member. Select several professionals to visit—there should be no charge for an introductory discussion. Make sure that whatever information they need to assist you is available for them.

Follow a similar procedure when choosing a counselor. Call several and make introductory visits. Ask questions about their experience with group work, family problems associated with small or family business, and background in understanding business problems. They might provide you with names of current or previous clients with situations similar to your own. Be sure to ask about their fee schedule.

Some Problems Never Go Away

Robert took our conversation about communication, cooperation and control to heart. Right away he set about organizing a board of directors, establishing a newsletter and suggestion box, and setting up regular monthly meetings with family members.

He called a staff meeting with the supervisors and then, with their assistance, met with each operating unit of the company. At the meeting Robert explained his philosophy of business, some of the goals he hoped to achieve and then asked for their suggestions for improvements, changes or reasons to stay with the status quo. Realizing that employees may not wish to be singled out in front of others, he recommended that they put all their ideas in the suggestion box with a *small bonus* and *personal recognition* in the newsletter for the best new ideas. Within the first month, the box was full and Robert decided this would be an ongoing part of office communication.

Organizing the board of directors took some thought. Robert wanted to benefit from the best advice he could find. He defined its purpose as a sounding board for decisions regarding company policy, planning and financial considerations. Its membership would include himself, his mother, his sister, Wayne, and one other supervisor as voting members. The company attorney and accountant would serve as advisors. This, Robert felt, would provide the critical feedback he needed to make mature and reasonable business decisions. The board decided to meet at least twice per year.

After the first monthly status meeting with the family, Robert realized that what he thought were minor issues of communication, cooperation and control were not as simple as he had expected. This had seemed an easy way to present his family with an update about profit and loss, volume of business and minor problems within the company. What he heard were a multitude of demands and concerns—not only about how the business was functioning but how each family member fit into the operation.

A few days after this meeting, Robert called for an appointment. "I thought I had it all figured out," he said. "After our last session I was going to start right into settling issues with my family. What I assumed would make everyone happy was not at all what they expressed in our meeting." He needed assistance in fulfilling their needs while maintaining control of the company.

Dealing With a Nonparticipatory Parent

Very often when a business owner passes away, control of the company is left to the spouse and many times the spouse is unprepared to deal with the problems and issues related to the day-to-day operations of the company. Since the business is usually the mechanism for providing an ongoing standard of living, it can become quite uncomfortable for the spouse not knowing how to make small or major business-related decisions. In many instances these issues will come at a time when the spouse is expecting to retire or is in the midst of their own worklife transition.

Realize that your parent is going through a period of confusion, pain and concern about the future. The business management team has only a vague awareness of the spouse's feelings since they are busily engaged in the company. Often their communication with your parent may be cursory and circumspect. In order to keep the parent from reacting with anxiety, ask the management team to establish regular meetings to discuss company status with a balance of good news and bad. Until a decision can be reached about what to do with the company, it is important for the parent to know in depth as much information as possible.

Provide every opportunity for your parent to become involved in management decision-making. Once the parent gains confidence that the administration is being handled with competence and professionalism, there will be less day-to-day stress and anxiety.

Your Turn

Answer the following:

► Does your parent feel the need to be involved?

► List five ways you can involve your parent in decision-making.

You Can Do It!!!

When a parent wants to become involved in the family business because they feel the need to protect themselves, provide every opportunity for them to play a role in the running of the company. Ask for assistance from your accountant or lawyer to develop a plan that will insure the continuity of the company and peace of mind for your parent.

Robert wanted to include his mother in whatever business activities he could even though once he acquired her stock he was under no legal requirement to do so, however apprehension about his own status and performance with the company didn't make him comfortable about including her in company affairs. "Maybe her needs and desires are overstated," he commented. "It's possible that she really only wants a level of involvement that would enable her to keep the benefits she became accustomed to with my dad. She always liked to go to lunch with the secretary to hear about office activities. She and dad took advantage of the supplier incentive programs, and dad always used the business to take care of her car. I know she needs to stay on the insurance plan to help pay some of her medical costs."

Robert's relationship with his mother was amiable, but Grace and Rachel had not developed much of a friendship even when the children were around. He described it as cordial but distant. Grace'srelationship with employees at the shop was friendly and social. "I really think she wants to do the right thing," he said, "only I don't believe she knows the issues, the practices or the reasoning for how a lot of things were done by my dad."

It seemed there was an issue of propriety here. His mother was, perhaps, confused—thinking she has to be close to everything in the business to protect her interests.

I told Robert about Cheryl and her husband's sporting goods store. When Calvin passed away he left a well-run and profitable full-range sporting good store. Though not a paid full-time employee, Cheryl was a part of the business by helping where useful.

Cheryl was in her mid 60s when Calvin died of cancer. The long-term illness had drained her of any enthusiasm for the business. Feeling there was a good management team in place, Cheryl took six weeks off to visit her children. At a loss as to where to focus her attention upon her return, she decided to find a place in the business to make up for her loneliness. Cheryl asked the sales manager and accountant to meet with her so she could find a place for herself without causing too much disruption in their day-to-day activities. They tried to talk her out of her plan. They felt the business was stable and productive and really didn't need additional help, but they arranged a position for her that would give her flexibility to come and go as she pleased.

Cheryl agreed to their suggestions. After a while, however, she became concerned about the conversations she was hearing. She overheard discussions about customer service policy, hiring and firing practices and attitudes about suppliers with which she didn't agree. She asked to meet with the management team to discuss their philosophies concerning the treatment of staff and customers. They were amused at her attitude and explained that in business you had to "be first" and "be tough." This meant that you had to aggressively pursue customers whatever the cost, allow exchanges only as a last resort and hire and fire until you found the right person regardless of personal differences.

That was not the way Cheryl felt a company should be managed. From there, a heated discussion caused management and owner to each retreat further into their positions. The managers felt that you shouldn't tamper with success. Cheryl felt her more humanitarian approach to business was better, even if there was a slimmer profit margin by being nice to customers. Although Cheryl had the power as owner to fire the management team, she had lost the desire to deal with all the problems this would entail. She felt too old to start over again by herself and sold the store to the managers to let them operate it however they wanted.

Making a Family Member Feel More Involved

How can you make a family member feel welcome in the company? Here are some ideasyou might try.

1. Schedule regular meetings with the family at the office to go over financial reports.

2. Provide copies of important correspondence for review.

3. Invite the family member to dine with customers and suppliers.

4. Inform the family member of supplier relations, pricing and policy.

5. Make company donations to the community in the family name.

6. Put family members on payroll to keep their health insurance current whenever possible.

7. Provide insurance and maintenance for an absentee owner's car whenever possible.

8. Keep supplier incentive programs available to family members.

"I think the cost would be minimal to the company," Robert said, "and these ideas should be enough to make my mother still feel a part of the operation of the business. Certainly none of these would interfere in my control of daily activities." He asked if these agreements should be made legally binding for her to feel that they would continue no matter what the circumstances. I told him that having a formal agreement would not be in the best interests of either party. Grace could bring to the board of directors any and all issues unresolved. If she had reservations about these matters, they would receive a fair hearing from the board.

Robert felt comfortable with this plan. He knew that leaving his mother out of the business entirely, even if she didn't have voting control with stock ownership, would not be in her best interest or the company's. A good portion of Grace's self-esteem was tied to the business; to remove her from this position abruptly would leave her not only struggling with the new role of widow, but totally disconnected from so much of her former life with Allen. Robert hoped that, as time passed, Grace would find other activities to fill this need. He realized, too, that Grace still had a lot to contribute to the company, especially as a family advisor. Her years with Allen had given her a perspective or "history" that was still of great value in planning the direction of the business.

Providing for Your Children—and Your Own Retirement

Concurrent with my work with Robert, I entered a professional relationship with another family interested in buying an existing business. Early one morning I got a call from Blair Abbott who resided in Bristol, Connecticut. He had heard about me from his daughter, who had attended a luncheon where I had given a talk about family business planning.

EXAMPLE

Blair Abbott took a retirement option from his employer, an electrical manufacturing company, whose largest customer was scaling down because of the economy. His retirement package included an impressive cash settlement and medical insurance coverage for two years. He and his wife, Debra, were in their mid-fifties and believed they were too young to stop working.

Their daughter Amanda was divorced and the mother of two preteenagers. She was thinking about the future, especially college for the children. Amanda was interested in starting a business of her own that would provide a creative challenge for herself and steady income to secure her children's education. She also wanted flexible hours that she could schedule around the children's activities. With her father's early retirement, she and he began thinking that a business could meet all their needs.

Blair thought that he and Debra could invest their cash settlement in a small business, hiring Amanda and training her to eventually run the operation. Amanda would buy out their interest when they really wanted to retire, providing a retirement income for Blair and Debra. It would also provide for Amanda's future as well as income she needed for a college fund for her children.

There was no reason to suggest a test to measure Blair's interest, attitude or commitment to own a business. It was apparent from the beginning that he and Debra agreee about what they wanted, and that Amanda was a significant part of their plan. All I was required to do as a counselor was help them address their unspoken concerns and establish time frames.

Checklist

❏ A board of directors can act as a forum to establish company goals, policy and financial matters.

❏ In a family business no one ever feels that personal issues are trivial.

❏ You can use the business to help with personal needs: insurance, car repairs, payroll.

❏ Fear and poor communication can invite unnecessary intervention.

❏ It's important to develop an atmosphere of accessibility and free yourself of controversy.

ASK YOURSELF

▶ How is the business set up to provide for the needs of a nonparticipatory parent?

▶ How do you plan on settling family arguments, long standing disputes and possible sibling rivalries?

▶ What avenue of communication have you provided for amongst the family?

CHAPTER
SIX

PROVIDING
A PLACE FOR
AN IMMEDIATE
RELATIVE

IS IT ALL ABOARD OR BON VOYAGE?

When you consider involving a relative in a paid position within a family business, be aware of the effect the decision will have not only on you, but the business and other employees. First, make sure that the hiring is based on company needs, not just a "make work" position to appease family. Don't create a situation that would alienate the relative in a hostile environment and strain company resources to provide for an unproductive or unnecessary employee.

Can you be unbiased about praise, work standards and expectations? For instance, will having your daughter near you every day create a stress that carries home after work? Will you be as tolerant of a relative's mistakes as you would be of another employee's? Can you treat your son with mature respect, instead of still thinking of his misdeeds as a teenager? If you don't apply the same standards to your relations as to your other employees, you run the risk of diluting respect others have for you in the workplace.

You need to be aware of your employee's reaction to hiring from among the family. They will be concerned how this person may effect them and wonder if the relative will pose a challenge to their role in the company. This is especially true if the relative enters at a management level. Employees will also wonder if they will be held accountable for the same standards, promotions and pay status as other nonfamily employees.

Your Turn

Answer the following:

▶ List five reasons why you should hire your relatives.

▶ List five reasons why you should not hire your relatives.

Take all the time you can before making a decision about hiring a relative. Be certain that you need another worker, that compensation for the position is on a par with everyone else's and that you will evaluate progress and competence on the same basis as you do other employees.

You Can Do It!!!

Write down your concerns about the decision to bring an immediate family member into the business, share them with your managers and look for ways to receive feedback about the possibilities. If you have already hired a relative, *have another manager be responsible* for the direct supervision and evaluation so that you can remain impartial. If all these conditions can be met, hiring a relative may be a good idea. Remember that "family loyalty" is a two-way street: employing your relation may be advantageous for both of you.

Siblings

"Next," Robert said, "I want to settle the involvement of my sister in the company. Janis has expressed an interest in full-time employment." Robert knew his sister had every right to be active in the company since she now owned a share of it. "What should I do?" he said.

This area is very sensitive. Robert should not try to take care of too many people with the company resources, especially those who might not contribute their full share. Before any decisions are made, Robert should look at the operating budget and see if any new employees are needed.

Even though Robert has a greater than 50% stake in the company, he has an obligation to the other owners to provide for their interests. To avoid a costly mistake, Robert must take a measure of Janis's true interest. Sharing detailed information about the company with his sister before resolving her employment may help strengthen his decision.

"I don't mind doing that," Robert said. "It's just that my sister is a political scientist by interest and training, and I can't see how her skills will benefit the cabinet business in any way."

Robert didn't think Janis was really interested in the business, but saw this as an opportunity for herself and wanted to capitalize on it. If she had the money she wanted, she might choose to do something else.

"She's really a talented craftsperson, Robert said. "She has often expressed a desire to open a quilt and needlework shop."

In this case, the cabinet company could invest capital in a needlework business in a small shopping center. The company could also supply some operating capital for the first 18 months through a note at a favorable rate of interest. If this was seen as an investment opportunity, Robert felt the board and his mother would be very supportive of this concept.

This was an alternative for his sister to benefit from the company without participating in the daily operations. It would also allow her to do something she had wanted to do for a long time. She could make some money on her own while having the fun of investing in a lifelong dream.

Thus Robert had peace of mind that he was using the business resources to help his sister while making money for the company.

Hiring Your Child Is Sometimes a Mistake

Sometimes involving a relative in the business doesn't work, as it didn't for Maria and her mother.

EXAMPLE

Maria's mother was divorced and had started her own company after working for someone else for 12 years. She employed seven people in sales, installation and bookkeeping.

Maria graduated from high school, but she decided she didn't want to go on to the local community college. She had planned all through high school to work for her mother and someday own the business. Unfortunately, several other employees felt they had a future for themselves in the company and were wary of Maria's interest. When she came to work, her mother started her out at the receptionist desk. This wasn't the job Maria thought she deserved, but decided to try it out to show everyone what she could do.

Her mother learned rather quickly that Maria didn't have any telephone skills, and she sent her to a local seminar for telephone practices. Maria showed some improvement, but would sometimes forget to take detailed messages or realize the importance of her response to customers. She often made personal calls. Her mother wasn't happy with her behavior, so she moved her to bookkeeping where she would handle customer calls and follow up on late accounts. She was more bored in this position than ever and asked her mother to try her out in sales or someplace exciting. Instead, mom told her to shape up or she was going to lose her job.

Eventually, Maria left for another position. The one she found provided more training, supervision and the challenge Maria wanted. With Maria working someplace else, mother and daughter got along better. The phone company employees were glad Maria had left because they resented helping a person who didn't view the value of a job as sensitively as they did.

Robert decided that unless he reoriented Janis to other interests, she might always need his attention. It is easy with a family member to forget that your purpose is to operate a successful business.

Hiring an Experienced Friend

Robert felt relieved. His mother and sister both knew how they would stay involved in the business and he was sure they would cooperate. Now the only remaining family member with a vested interest, and who might want some involvement, was his brother Steve. Robert thought his brother would be his toughest challenge because he was a successful regional manager of a food distribution service located in another state.

Steve, who was proficient in business matters, was the only family member to be concerned about the financial continuation of the company. He knew that if the business failed, he and the other children would be required to assist Grace financially, and, with his own growing family responsibilities, he didn't want this as an issue in the future. Robert had been so optimistic in buying the business he had refused to look at the possible negative side of family business ownership. Steve wanted to know his liability if financial conditions changed and bills couldn't be paid. He was also concerned about any contingent liabilities, such as insurance payments, retirement fund payouts and product warranty. In many ways he sounded more prepared to manage a business like this than was Robert. They had many long distance telephone calls trying to reach a comfort level for both of them.

Steve said he didn't want much to do with the business if he weren't actively involved. If his concerns about his liability could be resolved, he was willing to act in a benign fashion and simply share in his portion of the profits. He agreed to serve in an advisory capacity to Robert when needed, as long as it was friendly and unofficial. Robert also requested that Steve be active on the board to share in the long-range planning of the company.

This was a fair approach and Robert only needed to write Steve a letter outlining the details. He was enthusiastic to have Steve as a confidant and thought his influence would be helpful in maintaining a conservative course for the company's interest.

Robert was learning that family would be a major part of managing the cabinet business whether he liked it or not. Here's a checklist of what Robert learned to far.

Robert now knew that he needed to react to family interests swiftly and strongly or he would end up spending much of his time resolving trivial and troublesome issues.

Sometimes family members feel they have a right to be involved whether the company needs them or not. Robert hoped now that with some planning and discussion he could keep these matters from recurring, and was confident that he was looking out for their best interests.

Checklist

❏ Be aware that differences in management philosophy can draw a retired owner back into the business.

❏ Relatives sometimes feel they can demand unearned benefits from the business.

❏ Plans to employ a family member should include every step you would take for hiring everyone else.

❏ Flexibility is important when bringing family members into the business. They make mistakes too.

❏ Sometimes family members won't work out in the business. If not, follow established procedure.

❏ Don't jeopardize the company trying to meet family demands.

ASK YOURSELF

► Which family members might expect to work for or be involved with the business and in what capacity?

► How have you prepared to negotiate with family members about their involvement?

► Describe the benefits of establishing a board of directors, including family members, for your company.

CHAPTER SIX

CHAPTER
SEVEN

I LOVE YOU
DEARLY,
BUT. . .

MARRIAGE IN A FAMILY BUSINESS

Robert ran into a problem when Janis decided she would rather work in the business than open a needlecraft shop. He ran into a second problem when Rachel wanted a job, too. The company couldn't provide the work to accommodate them.

Janis wanted variable hours so she could be home in the afternoon when her children returned from school. She said she wanted to get involved in the family business so that one day maybe one of her children could work there. She also wanted to protect her interests and felt this would only be accomplished if she could see first hand what was happening.

Robert wasn't too concerned about his nieces or nephews. They were still young and they wouldn't be interested in working for several years. But he did need to resolve what to do with his sister. Where could he possibly find a place for her?

A counselor can help in this situation. I offered to talk with Janis and interview her about her career plans. This would be similar to the testing I had conducted with Robert when he first approached me about buying the company. With the results of the tests and follow-up discussion with Janis, I thought we could find the appropriate place for her to contribute to the company. I urged him to keep an open mind about this. The possibility was good that she could become a productive employee. He agreed, but wasn't all that convinced that a solution could be found that would fit his needs.

Creating an Employee Profile

Janis understood Robert's reticence about her involvement with the company, but she had decided that this was a perfect opportunity to learn new skills, earn some money and be an integral part of the family business. Her attitude was positive. She was willing to live with the policies of the company and didn't want to be treated differently from anyone else, except she wanted a flexible schedule to allow her to be home when the children arrived in the afternoon. Janis didn't think this was so strange a request and planned to prevail on her status with the family to get what she wanted.

In her political science major at college, Janis did extensive library research and statistical analysis. She believed her sense of organization and planning were helpful in getting excellent grades in her major course of study. Summer jobs and an administrative aide position in government taught her how to work independently, think quickly on her feet and ask for what she wanted. She was certain that if she had not met John and married, she would have continued her education all the way to a doctorate. She had never worked in a business before, but felt confident that her career skills could be applied to any working situation.

Janis was skeptical about what the test scores might reveal. She didn't think this process could really tell her anything new, but she agreed to the testing because it seemed to be important to Robert.

The test results showed a convincing match between her interests and personality: she preferred to work alone, had a mechanical aptitude and could be content working in a scientific endeavor. She enjoyed working with numbers and statistics. These were a few of her major interests and personality traits that gave her cause to think about which career direction she wanted to take.

"What does this mean to my brother, the company and my place in it?" Janis asked. We discussed how the company could use her interests in statistics, data analysis and computers. "Maybe this is a way to keep you sharp and interested in some of your career goals. What if you designed a computer model for the company to integrate all its management and service functions and develop a comprehensive reporting format by working with the supervisors in their areas of expertise? If you could produce a cost analysis for jobs in progress and completed jobs, just think about how Robert could make needed changes to improve profitability. With your home computer you could do this on a contract basis and only need to go to the office periodically. You could develop and administer training programs for the staff and everyone could become computer literate. While doing this," I added, "you could get paid for your time and efforts, or enroll in a class at the university if you want."

Janis thought this was a plan that suited her and she agreed to talk it over with Robert. She was excited that what she learned about herself would tie into future plans for when the children were older. Now she felt she had a clear path to follow.

Robert and Janis later worked out an arrangement similar to what she and I had discussed. They decided to have Janis research computer applications in the cabinet industry and create the family business newsletter. According to Robert, she was enthusiastic and settled on what was to happen for at least the new few years. He would pay her a suitable hourly rate and put her on the company insurance policy.

What to Consider When Bringing Relatives into the Family Owned Business

Some basic suggestions can lay a good framework for opening a business to family members. If you view these hints from the standpoint of a teacher who will mold and model their learning experiences, you can expect a work ethic you want that will reflect your style.

1. *Treat business as a learning experience.* Since you are the manager-owner, there won't be anyone else who knows the answer better than you. As people learn and grow, they accumulate successes and translate them into confidence, which enables them to make the best decisions in your interests. Think about how to bring learning experiences into the workplace as a means of upgrading skills and providing an environment where new approaches to your business can be applied. While this process is as meaningful to any new employee, it will allow a relative to work for you in your best interests.

2. *Expect mistakes.* If you approach relatives in a business expecting them to perform in an unrealistic manner, you will neither help them or your relationship. Your relatives should be treated like any other employee. There will be a period when you wonder if they will master the pricing system or paper routing. The investment you make will pay dividends many times over. Don't forget that you went through some rough times learning your business, too.

3. *Let everyone know what's happening.* Family business owners are conservative and keep a lot of what they know to themselves. My father kept important information in little slips of paper that he stuck in his shirt pocket, back pants pocket and over the visor of his pickup truck. It was common for him to take all his pieces of paper out and spread them on the table to check on a quote or locate a phone number. He had a secretary and several men performing jobs for him. Many times I heard complaints about not knowing information because he had it written down somewhere but no one else knew where to find it.

4. *Provide feedback on a regular basis.* Since one of your purposes may be to have a successor ready to take over in an emergency, it's useful to have a relative knowledgeable about your work. Training meetings can be expanded to allow for an exchange of ideas and opinions, which can provide a good forum for teaching your business philosophy and how you expect it to be carried out.

5. *Give your relative a piece of your domain to manage.* Since the purpose is to teach readiness for expanded duties, look for increased competence and interest so you will know what is needed to make changes in their duties. If the interest isn't there, you've still learned valuable information about the person with little commitment on your part. I've seen only a few instances where this hasn't worked. Manny let his son handle the trucks in his linen supply business. He was to keep all the maintenance records and report the repairs. His son did such a good job that the company next door, a surveyor's office, contracted with Manny to conduct maintenance and repairs on their vehicles as well.

6. *Evaluate your relative on the same basis as any other employee.* Feedback on their job status is essential. To learn how they perform in relation to others in the same job will be helpful for your peace of mind and their morale. Be honest in your appraisal, because others in the company are watching to see what you do. There is nothing wrong with having high expectations of a relative, just don't

let your emotions get out of hand. Few employees like to see a relative exploited. If respect from your employees is important to you, your fairness in this domain is essential.

7. *Allow your relative time alone in their area of interest.* This way they can learn what to do without your assistance. After all, your goal is to prepare them to do their job without your help. Giving them the freedom to perform for their own benefit enhances their growth.

"Remember Robert," I said, "you're the teacher and you have to think all the time about what it is you want a relative to learn on the job. If you model what you want, you'll get it back twofold. People learn how to do things in a lot of different ways. Subtle meanings may be missed or misrepresented leading to confusion."

Your Turn

Answer the following:

► Which of the seven considerations for bringing relatives into a family-owned business affect you the most? The best?

Marriage in a Family Business

In a business setting, roles are designed to flow in authority from the top down. This means that the owner is the public, decision-making figure and all other positions are supportive. Unless the spouse has a position in the company of responsibility equal to the owner (which might occur for two professionals working together), one person will be in a subordinate role. For the owner to treat his or her spouse any differently from other employees opens the door for criticism from all sides. Therefore, when critique of job performance or extra demands are placed on the spouse, hurt feelings and misunderstandings can arise. You often take your business frustrations with the job or the boss home with you, but it's not so easy to do when you face the source of your anger across the dinner table.

You will find business talk with your spouse becoming part of daily life. Social activities, friends, family outings all start to revolve around the company and its needs and demands. Owning and managing a family business has enough long hours without extending business time to the few hours at home, too. This has a cumulative effect on a couple, so that silently each person may start to chose sides about what is more important, marriage and family or the business and its boss/subordinate relationship.

You Can Do It!!!

If employing your spouse in the family business is your decision, take all the time you need to discuss and plan. Arrange your space at work and at home to provide for alone time for each of you. Establish a buffer between you at work, physically and mentally. Try to have your spouse report to someone else. Be clear that business concerns are only discussed at home for a certain period of time (maybe at dinner only, or during a before-dinner drink) or set a "meeting" time each week to hash out any business concerns. Stick with this schedule as much as possible so it doesn't interfere with the rest of the family time together. Establish time for play and recreation that doesn't involve any business affairs.

Calming Apprehensions

Robert was apprehensive about his wife being an active part of the business. For the past several years, Rachel had enjoyed being an elementary school teacher. Their living and work arrangement had been satisfactory and there had been few problems caring for the children, caring for the family and finding time for each other.

Now, Rachel was worried that she wouldn't be able locate the kind of teaching position she wanted. If she could have a choice she would work in a school district close to home. But if she had to spend a lot of time commuting, she was concerned that she'd lose the time she normally spent with the family.

Rachel was feeling some resentment about having to leave her job in exchange for the risk they were taking with the cabinet company. Part of her thinking was that if she could not find the ideal job, then she would ask Robert to create a job for her. She wasn't really concerned about what she would do in the office, she just felt that a paid position was due her since she had given up so much of what she wanted. She told Robert that working in the cabinet company would enable her to be available to the children and help with the extra expenses of living in a larger city.

Robert's concerns were justified. Even if he were president of the corporation, it would be difficult for him to feel comfortable in the workplace with Rachel around all the time. There probably would be little controversy with his sister on staff because she went home to her own family, but Rachel would not. Rachel might be viewed as an interloper and a threat to the social balance of internal operations.

In-Law Conflicts

These issues pale next to the problem it would create with Robert's mother. Rachel and Grace were not close. They had conflicting personalities, and neither would ever consider accounting to the other for their actions. Grace now felt a real proprietary relationship with the company. With Robert at the helm, she felt secure and protected, and he enjoyed a sense of power she never had when her husband was in charge.

This situation is common in families where a succession plan has not been developed. Now Grace had a great deal of power and control and no practical knowledge of what this meant.

Spouse or Employee

Rachel and I discussed all the issues Robert and I had explored, and she agreed to go through a testing program. At issue was whether she could be integrated into the daily operations of the company without disrupting other employees and their jobs. Would she require a great deal of training to learn the skills she needed?

Rachel's test results showed that she liked to work in groups, her career interests were strongly oriented toward young children and she was very sensitive to criticism. She explained that she would prefer teaching at the elementary school level, but she hadn't done much about looking for a teaching job. She had been too busy with the move and setting up another home. We worked on a plan for how she would find the teaching job she wanted and agreed to give the task six months before she'd talk to Robert about a job with the company. After working on a resume, cover letter and related aspects of a job search, she agreed to meet with Robert and me.

Spouses and Hierarchies

Spouses get involved in their partners' businesses in a lot of different ways. Some couples start out working together or, at a later point in the marriage, the spouse comes into the office. Whatever the configuration, the parnters rarely achieve a status of equality in the workplace. One of them is always the boss, and then they have to go home and resume a more equal relationship. Achieving this balance is difficult.

Robert thought that having Rachel working fulltime with the business was not desirable. He felt he wouldn't be able to be himself with Rachel around all the time. She didn't have the same reservation, but thought their personality differences in working with people would clash. Rachel said Robert liked telling people what to do, whereas she liked leaving people alone to do their job. Men and women often communicate differently, and this needs to be understood by couples who work together.

Sex Differences in Communicaton Styles

I said these are exactly the issues they needed to express. "Also," I said, "there's a difference in how you both communicate as man and woman that help explain some of these sources of conflict." In our culture we've conditioned men to behave in a certain manner and women in another. It's typical for a husband to come home from work and spend 15 or 20 minutes talking about his day. This is his method of communication. When he's finished with the subject, he wants no more to do with it. Meanwhile he hears a little of his partner's day and considers the day's debriefing over. He isn't aware that his wife is processing what she has been told and has a few questions. When her husband said he told someone off that's all he wants to say about it. Later in the evening, his wife will ask the inevitable question, "So what did he say after you told him off?" Now the husband has had his television interrupted and the last thing he wants to do is discuss ancient history. This keeps up for a few minutes, and then he explodes. He's finished talking, and she wants to know some of the details. Now they are both upset. He can't understand why she is still talking about the issue. She believes he lacks insight into her feelings. They go to bed mad only to have a similar scene repeat itself time and again. A good book on this is *That's Not What I Meant and You Just Don't Understand* by Deborah Tannen, Ballantine Books, 1987, for a thorough exploration of how men and women miscommunicate. There is also a book by Loughary and Ripley called *Working It Out Together, a Guide For Duel Career Couple,* New Directions, 1987. This text discusses how to organize their career and family lives.

How to Keep Harmony in the Marriage

Couples can increase their chances for working harmoniously together. These ideas are tough but negotiable.

> ► *Money is never a substitute for love or family.* Don't confuse business with a way of life. Other jobs can be found. Maybe the income will be reduced and lifestyle different, but the family should be the focus of your efforts. Never tell your spouse, "I'm doing this for the family." Your spouse knows better.

▶ *If your spouse plans to work with you, leave your work at the office.* Think about how creative you can become to keep business problems where they belong. We've all seen too many marriages come apart because work stress finds its way into the relationship. Certainly the union is based on other interests besides the business. To keep the marriage fresh and alive, leave all business talk at the company and concentrate on other activities at home.

▶ *Don't forget to have fun.* It's easy to lose perspective in your lives if all you do is get up, go to work, go to bed and keep repeating the cycle. This has its obvious disastrous consequences.

▶ *Don't let outside family concerns interfere.* If Rachel is to be involved in the business, Grace can have no authority over her. If Grace doesn't like something she sees, she takes the problem to Robert, not to Rachel. This rule applies just as it would with any other employee concern.

▶ *A commitment to the marriage is of prime importance.* Without this "glue," the relationship cannot be expected to remain intact if problems arise.

▶ *Decisions must be made by both partners.* Communication will maintain a cooperative spirit and ensure that both feel they are partners, without anyone being put in a subordinate role.

▶ *Division of labor can overcome sources of stress.* However family and household responsibilities are shared, all family members should agree on this division of labor. Unlike a business, there is no boss and employee relationship at home. All members are coworkers who share the job.

▶ *Define and clarify job descriptions.* Chances are, if both partners are professionals, both need to maintain their independence. If the roles are boss and subordinate, clarify that all parties are comfortable with this arrangement.

Putting It All Together

These factors may not be inclusive, but if Robert thinks about each one as it relates to his situation, it might help him decide what to do about Rachel joining him in business. He thought if he were more supportive of Rachel's teaching career, she might realize it's what she wants, too.

By now Robert knew that hiring relatives means more than just putting them on payroll. Because being part of a family is so complex, it is sometimes difficult to maintain resolve and have strength in your judgments.

Business Conflict Situations

1. SITUATION

Art manages the family wholesale appliance business. Business is slow, and he has laid off two employees. His sister has just called, asking him to hire her 16-year-old son, who is having trouble in school. She says that if her son doesn't have a job, he may have to go into juvenile detention. What should Art say to his sister?

PROPOSED RESOLUTION

Family businesses are often viewed as a panacea to family problems. Art doesn't have to hire his nephew, but in the spirit of helping his sister he may want to bring his nephew on board. The complications that result may be greater than he wants to handle. He might best serve his family if he talks to a friend who may be able to hire his sister's son, which would let him monitor the nephew's progress without the problems of direct supervision.

2. SITUATION

Your brother, five years younger than you, is employed in your paper products company. You've just discovered that he's written a check for $3,000 to himself. When you ask him about it, he tells you he needs the money to pay for the boat he bought that they can't afford. He offers to pay the money back over time if he can borrow it now, but you are suspicious of his sincerity. What do you do?

PROPOSED RESOLUTION

Money in family businesses is always a source of controversy. The brother's spending habits do not concern to the family business. To allow this breach of trust and policy would be wrong for the company. A principal may justify loaning the money, but it will likely result in another request before too long. The company would be better off not to allow the loan.

SITUATION

Marty and June have a pest control business. On the job he is Mr. Perfect to everyone, always full of compliments and helpful advice. At home, especially after a few drinks, he's loud, coarse and rough, always belittling June and the kids whatever they do. What should June do?

PROPOSED RESOLUTION

Husbands and wives working together in the family business an always a risk. There are problems enough in the day-to-day management of the enterprise without confronting the emotions of spouses on and off the job. In this case, June could benefit from discussing her situation with a counselor and developing a plan for how to cope with her husband in both settings. It would be even more beneficial to her if she could persuade him to seek counseling with her. If the business depends on her services or skills and financially the company needs to rely on her employment, chances are good that her husband will attempt to remedy his behavior for the sake of the company, if not his marriage.

SITUATION

Dave owned a printing business when he met Linda. She was his bookkeeper and after a few years of dating, they got married. It didn't take long for the accounting manager to notice that her work attitude had changed. Linda now assumed she could get away with whatever she wanted to do as the boss's wife, which caused friction in the office. How should the accounting manager approach Linda without alienating her?

PROPOSED RESOLUTION

Office staff and administrators are very conscious about the presence of the boss's spouse on the job. When this matter becomes troublesome—especially with an alienating attitude by the spouse—the entire office staff can become demoralized. Any competent businessperson should be made aware when unfair practices by family members are displayed. In this case, the accounting manager needs to make an appointment with the owner as soon as possible to explain what is occurring in that department. It's essential that this attitude and behavior be addressed as quickly as possible. The overall impact will be a more harmonious work setting.

5. SITUATION

You've been an active owner-manager of a business machine company since you graduated from college 20 years ago. Now that your youngest son has left for university, your husband is exploring new career ideas for himself. He's suggested that he work from your office to provide an executive office decorating service. You think it is a good idea, but your brother, who came to work for the company a few years ago, gives the idea an emphatic "no." Your husband is convinced that his idea should be given a chance. How can you find a solution to this controversy?

PROPOSED RESOLUTION

Lots of good ideas go by the wayside because someone in the family business doesn't want to accept them. Blocking the implementation of good ideas because they come from a certain member of the family can be counterproductive and hurtful. This issue has no easy resolution and could create long-term problems in business and the marriage. In this case the wife is in a tough spot. She may believe in her husband's ideas, but not strongly enough to challenge her brother. She needs to identify her husband's and brother's individual needs and find out if her brother has an irrational emotional response. She also needs to find out where her own loyalties lie and make the decision based on its effect on everyone involved.

ASK YOURSELF

▶ Discuss the effect on your marriage if you and your spouse worked together.

- What would the effect be on the rest of your immediate family?

- Comment on your ability to treat your spouse as you would another employee.

CHAPTER EIGHT

FAMILY MEMBERS ARE LIKE OTHER EMPLOYEES

AN OBJECTIVE VIEW IS REQUIRED

Getting family members settled into the day-to-day routine of the business is a major achievement. Find ways to orient them to the profitability of the company. Robert had worked hard to help Janis and Rachel develop their best interests as well as those of the company. Great effort had been expended to match their interests, experiences, training and ability.

Robert was benefiting from the planning we had done. Everyone had settled into a routine, and he was finally finding the time to handle management concerns, such as increasing market share and implementing a new computer graphics program to help with estimating. Robert was starting to feel competent in this business and it was beginning to be fun.

FAMILY MEMBERS ARE EMPLOYEES

Then Robert's brother-in-law, Ron, arrived in town with his two kids. They are temporarily living with Robert and Rachel until Ron can figure out what to do after his divorce. He's a great guy and a heck of a salesman, but he doesn't know a thing about the cabinet business. Robert could use a new salesman since Jim left, but he doesn't want to get obligated to him in any way. Still, Robert feels that the sooner Ron starts work, the sooner he'll get the house back into some kind of order.

Robert's major fear was that if he hired Ron, the rest of the sales staff would think he was playing family favorites. Janis, working parttime from home, had not caused employee resentment, but Ron would be the second family member Robert hired, and he would be highly visible in an in-house job. Though Ron didn't have a college degree, he had been in home appliance sales for the past 12 years. Since the company usually hired salesmen with some experience in construction, Robert was concerned that whatever precedent he established could be applied to all the sales staff. This would leave room for complaints from everyone involved.

Guidelines for Hiring Family Members

Here are some guidelines that might make sense in any new hire situation.

1. If the company cannot support any more employees, don't hire. (In this case, however, not only was the company trying to increase market share through expanded marketing but it was short of sales staff from the vacancy left by Uncle Jim.)

2. If the compensation scheme with Ron includes fringe benefits, an unrealistic base salary and liberal leave, a norm may be established that will irritate and anger other employees. Pay everyone the same.

3. View the person objectively. An unobjective advocate (in this case, Rachel) may be exerting influence. Although Ron may be an effective, professional salesperson to his sister Rachel, he will have to prove it to Robert.

Hidden Members on Payroll: Don't Risk It

I've worked with family businesses that have many family members on the payroll; however, only the accountant knew they were considered employees. My friend Ed kept his mother, wife and two daughters on his payroll for years. In addition, they had liberal company benefits such as health insurance, incentive trips and company car maintenance. In some cases, this may be warranted, such as maintaining health insurance on a company policy for an older family member like Grace, but it can cause a lot of ill feelings among employees who see the boss's relatives benefiting from their hard work. Make sure all paid family members have *real* jobs at a level consistent with their abilities and experience, with pay based on merit just like any other employee.

A Training Plan

Ron's training will be the key to his acceptance in the company. Good sales jobs have more to do with *internal support services* and *product training* than commission schedule and base salary. If Robert can produce a plan that will prepare Ron for cabinet sales, he can expect good results. These ideas will help Ron make the best use of his training period.

► Provide learning experiences throughout the production cycle that will build Ron's competence and confidence.

► Give Ron enough control over his sales domain to make decisions necessary for getting orders. Train him to exchange materials in a job, thereby cutting costs.

► Prepare Ron to make important financial commitments to his customers. For instance, if his customer needs 90 days to pay, Ron may need to put a carrying charge in the proposal.

Robert should reinforce his goal that service and quality are the customers' best measurement of company performance. As long as sales staff can count on high-quality construction and a continual upgrade of product, they will have effective results.

Cross-Training

I thought this might be a good time to talk to Robert about cross-training of employees. "I think this concept can be of great value to you," I told him. "What if you put together a plan whereby every person on staff learns the basics about someone else's job? When someone goes on vacation, someone else will know the rudiments of that job."

The principle in cross-training is to insure that important functions are performed in any contingency. Not only will this be effective in an emergency, but if your staff knows other aspects of the business, their overall understanding of the company will be enhanced. When the dispatcher learns the tasks of the billing clerk, the dispatcher then knows what steps are taken to prepare a billing, can check its accuracy and prepare a cost analysis of each job. The sales staff can learn data entry skills to perform this function by themselves.

Most of all, cross-training allows employees to take time when needed for advanced training and schedule vacations knowing their job will get done. Morale is an important factor, too. Breaks from routine provide opportunities to learn new skills and enhance an employee's value to the company. Someone may advance in the company once they have learned and performed other job skills.

Your Turn

Answer the following:

► List the areas in which your business can support another employee.

► What training will be required for the position?

Evaluating Relatives in a Family Business

A common criticism of family business owners is that they appear to give preferential treatment to family members on the job. While this may be warranted in a few cases, in general this practice leads to poor employee morale. To insure a respectful atmosphere between owner and employees, it is essential that the doctrine of fair treatment be administered at all levels of management.

The job evaluation process, in particular, is a problem that can divide family from other employees. There are standard formats for assessing the progress of employees, and these procedures should be followed explicitly with family members.

If possible, have the relative report to a manager other than yourself, alleviating bias and frustration. The manager can report to you if there are any problems with job performance or any changes needed in training or experience.

Acknowledge that the other employees may feel that in the long run they will not achieve the status awarded a relative of the owner—even if they perform in an equal and acceptable manner. In a nonunion company, the owners of a family business may make their promotions and hiring decisions based on their own desires. If a relative is brought into the company to be trained for a top management position (or ownership upon retirement), make this clear right away, so that employees who may have a personal involvement in this decision understand your desires. If everyone is honest from the beginning, questions and concerns can be addressed before a negative situation develops.

In the interests of thorough planning, it is a good idea to take notes of your meetings with all employees who may be involved in an evaluation process. This documentation will go a long way in convincing employees that you are serious about impartial judgments during the evaluation of a relative.

You Can Do It!!!

As you plan for your relative to learn the business, take time to bring in important employees who may be useful in training that person. Administer standardized tests and measures of job proficiency to gauge the learning process. Make open and public statements about your wanting a competent, dedicated employee in your relative and follow through by lending support to supervising staff.

Employee Assessment

The value of assessments is to let employees know where they stand at a certain time and in relationship to where they want to be. If a salesperson wishes to excel, needs to know if the sales goal has been met, or if the salespitch is on the right track—additional efforts in certain areas might achieve company or individual goals.

Robert wanted to know how he could rate the performance of his employees to know when a raise or promotion was justified (see Employee Assessment Form). One way is to rate the employees on a scale from one to five on the following measures. Because all components of a business are different, he could change any areas to accommodate his needs.

These general assessment variables may be expanded depending upon the job and business functions. For instance, evaluation of a management employee may emphasize commitment to company goals and adaptability rather than treatment of equipment or training. If an individual is being evaluated for a management team, personality criteria such as cooperativeness, may take on an elevated role.

Employee Evaluation Questionnaire

1. It is fairly easy to measure the results of a physical product, such as the construction of a cabinet, but how will you measure the accomplishments of support services, such as inventory control or receptionist duties? How could you set tangible goals for every employee to reinforce a sense of accomplishment?

2. Is the employee sufficiently challenged by the task? If not, could this be attained? When the task is varied and exercises the body and the brain, the result is more likely to be of consistently high quality and the worker will be more interested.

3. Does the staff know what levels of quality are expected? Confusion about what constitutes an acceptable product will delay production.

4. Do you provide training to help employees whose work is standard or substandard? Giving them the proper tools and assistance to do a job correctly will produce a high-quality product.

5. Do your jobs provide enough income for your employees to live independently and support a family? No one wants to work an eight-hour shift and yet not make enough to stay off public assistance. However, if an employee knows that a low-wage job will be a stepping stone to higher paying position, it may be an incentive to work hard and receive additional training.

6. Have you structured your tasks and job descriptions so that, with time and exemplary work performance, people can move up in the company?

Assessment Form

	Rating				
A. Job Performance					
1. Skills					
a. Verbal	1	2	3	4	5
b. Technical	1	2	3	4	5
2. Work habits					
a. Punctual	1	2	3	4	5
b. Completes tasks on time	1	2	3	4	5
3. Overall effectiveness	1	2	3	4	5
B. Personal Characteristics					
1. Communicates with coworkers	1	2	3	4	5
Communicates with managers	1	2	3	4	5
Communicates with customers	1	2	3	4	5
2. Assertiveness					
a. Uses initiative	1	2	3	4	5
b. Self starter	1	2	3	4	5
C. Adaptability					
1. Flexible	1	2	3	4	5
2. Cooperative	1	2	3	4	5
D. Treatment of Equipment					
1. Performs routine preventive maintenance	1	2	3	4	5
2. Notifies supervisor when repair is needed	1	2	3	4	5
3. Safety conscious	1	2	3	4	5

Assessment Form (continued)

	Rating
E. Commitment to Company Goals	
1. Alerts supervisor when job cost is out of line	1 2 3 4 5
2. Routinely evaluates job progress	1 2 3 4 5
3. Works within company policies	1 2 3 4 5
F. Willingness to Continue Training Education	
1. Takes advantage of training opportunities	1 2 3 4 5
2. Uses training and education to improve status with company	1 2 3 4 5

When evaluating a relative, it is wise to have staff member other than the owner-manager conduct the review. This is especially true with very close relatives like parents or spouse. Feedback on a relative's job performance is equally important as it is to anyone else in the company.

Your personal vision for the company may require that you establish your own loyal team inside the company who will help you translate your dream into reality. Look for people who can relate to your ideas. Asking relevant questions of key employees may help you refine what you want.

Recruit from Within the Company

When you must replace people because of retirement or other reasons, let employees know you want to hire internally. You may be surprised by who steps forward to show their interest.

A lot of positives can be accomplished by bringing someone in from the sales field or from product repair. Sales force expertise is of great value to everyone. Who bests knows about construction of a certain product or the most economical way to repair it than those who have had to do it themselves? These are ideal people to train others in the intricacies of production. A mentor relationship can produce benefits for a long time.

Many times management will look outside the company for employees only to decide that the best personnel resources are within the company. For example, an installer taken from the daily task of insulating can, with a bit of training, be an excellent choice to supervise field crews or estimate jobs.

EXAMPLE

Susan Bendix is president and CEO of an international consulting company. When she was an upcoming executive with her firm, she initiated a company policy of allowing CEOs and presidents to serve only through their 65th birthday. She was eloquent in her belief that for younger executives to stay with the company, they needed to know they had a chance to run the business someday. Now Susan (who just turned 65) is not happy she must retire, but with as much grace as she can muster, she is stepping down and training her successor.

Give Everyone A Chance to Advance

It is important to give everyone a chance to advance themselves. Even Wayne should be eligible to run the cabinet company if Robert's vision expands to other business interests. There is great value in planning ahead, since employees need to feel there is a place for them where they can produce for their own interests.

Performance Incentives

As an owner-manager, you must provide incentives that motivate employees and family members to do their best. Motivation to be on time, perform competitively and be considerate should be expected of all employees. There is much that can be done to keep job interest alive.

► One suggestion is to pay the full premium for health insurance for exemplary salespeople. This might be worth several hundred dollars a month to an employee, since most small companies have their employees contribute to their insurance plan.

► This same idea could be applied to long-term employees who might wish to continue with the insurance plan after retirement.

► Profit sharing has been a traditional incentive to maintain employees. When the company make money, a reasonable contribution can have far-reaching benefits. What better attraction for a company than to pay a percentage of an employee's salary at the end of the year into an account for their future?

► These sums can be substantial. Some people, after 10 years of profit sharing, accepted the penalty for early withdrawal and opened a company themselves.

There are dozens of ideas that motivate people. One non-monetary reward is to give a team one day off per month on a rotating basis if negotiated quotas or goals are met in production, sales or safety. Having an extra three-day weekend per month interests almost everyone.

Give employees some say in the company's policies. People like to feel their contributions are important.

Another factor is environment: Let employees give you an idea of needed space, tools, or decor items and implement these ideas.

Realize that this is a business not just for your vision, but can also be a means to help others carry out their dreams. If you can put some of these concerns to work with family and employees, combining with sensibility with sincerity, you can all enjoy a positive and prosperous adventure.

Motivation Checklist

❏ Have family members learn how they contribute to profitability.

❏ Once the basics of a business are mastered, ask for ideas for expansion.

❏ Remember that time and experience set the stage for competent management.

❏ Your company must have the funds before it can consider hiring family members.

❏ Use support systems and training. They can be as invaluable to relatives in the family business.

❏ Cross-training benefits everyone.

❏ Use personnel evaluation procedures for all employees, including family members.

❏ A team approach to management provides a support system for everyone.

❏ Think about the value of promoting from within.

❏ Give everyone a chance at your job through training, feedback and encouragement.

❏ Remember to think about who will replace you when you retire.

❏ Creative use of incentives will keep everyone interested in your company.

❏ Remember your employees and their families depend on you doing your job efficiently, too. Ask for feedback.

❏ Once your management team is in place, bring your long-range goals into focus through discussion.

ASK YOURSELF

► Discuss the methods you will use to keep your spouse and other family members informed about your plans.

► Describe the plan you have for cross-training your employees.

► What incentive or reward plans do you have set up for your employees?

CHAPTER
NINE

SUCCESSION PLANNING

IT'S NEVER TOO EARLY TO PLAN FOR THE FUTURE

So far Robert's arrangement with his brother Steve had been an asset to Robert. When he felt overwhelmed about business problems, Steve was just the person to be the voice of reason and offer suggestions. While this was a helpful arrangement, Steve lived miles away, so contact was infrequent. Now that Robert was more knowledgeable about his family business affairs, he wanted to find someone with whom he could debrief his day and talk about his immediate plans.

When Robert came into our next session he was satisfied that the cabinet shop had settled into a routine. I asked him how his brother-in-law was doing in the company. "That's probably my best move," he said. He described how the sales staff had rallied around Ron and sales were showing a major improvement.

"What would happen if for some reason you couldn't come into the office every day? Who would you want to manage the business, Ron or Wayne?" I asked.

"That's a good question," Robert said. "Wayne does a fine job and we get along all right; however, I've found I have more in common with Ron. If something happened to me, I'd feel more comfortable if he was in a position to protect my interests because he's family. He may not know the full range of management functions in this business yet, but I trust him."

"If you had to make a decision today between Wayne or Ron as your replacement, who would it be?" I asked. Robert had said before that he would like to grow beyond the cabinet making business and diversify into other areas sometime in the future. With less than one full year in charge, the question still seemed like one that should be asked.

Succession Planning

Succession issues require sophisticated planning so that whoever is chosen is the most qualified candidate. Every businessperson knows someone who has had to reenter a business because a relative made the erroneous assumption that the company was placed in good and qualified hands.

Sometimes a consultant chooses the successor. The consultant evaluates the candidates and presents a choice based on an analysis of what is good for the owner. The owner plans and implements the recommendations.

This sort of planning is most successful when the business owner is involved every step of the way. Typically, the longer the entrepreneur is in business, the more difficult it is to see the best candidate among the possibilities. All too often the process is executed subjectively or desperately.

Planning who is to succeed you is never a wasted effort. The idea is to assess the strengths and weaknesses of Ron and Wayne so that when Robert is ready to implement the succession plan, he will have a successful transition.

Goals of Succession Planning

The goal of succession planning is to find or prepare a person to do the owner's job without assistance. If the vital operating units of the company can be managed by someone else, the right person to follow the entrepreneur has been found. Robert realized that he needed another individual in his business to provide back up to his management in case of emergency. He was firm in his commitment to evaluate Ron and Wayne fairly. His circumstances do not fit the traditional parent-to-child succession of most small family-owned businesses.

Even if Robert had already made a decision about Wayne or Ron, this process would help sort out the levels of preparedness and competency for succession of each person. The first step is to assess their performance in four business management categories. Each dimension includes subsections that identify personal qualities, behaviors or attitudes important in determining the level of readiness in each category.

Your Turn

Answer the following:

► To which employees have you delegated important aspects of your business operation?

► Who is your likely successor in case you cannot continue to work?

► List five key sources of information within the organization for your successor.

► As part of the training for successor, have you planned for this person to contribute to decisions?

Management Decisions Important in Choosing a Successor

Some major management decisions will enable you to evaluate each possible successor. The range of data you may wish to collect about possible replacements can vary widely. When considering a son or daughter, your adherence to a formal outline may not be as rigorous as with other employees. Your aim should be to judge your candidates on their performance of tasks you do as owner-manager. Remember that the purpose of finding a qualified successor is to carry on the business without you.

If you have three or four successor candidates, it is important to give all equal consideration. This is the only way you can be certain that you've made the best choice among them. If a candidate lacks skills in one management area but performs well in all the others, that candidate shouldn't be eliminated. With proper training and experience, all of your choices can gain needed academic preparation and work experience to make them outstanding successor.

Consider management performance, leadership, technical ability and personal strengths in evaluating your candidates. It may be helpful to inform all of your potential choices that you are thinking about them as a successor. Discuss ways they could improve their experience or education to be ready to take over the business.

You Can Do It!!!

Draw up a list of qualifications for your successor. Decide how soon you want to make a choice and inform those under consideration. Explain the time constraints you are under and set deadlines for decisions along the way. It's likely that some candidates will drop out along the way, but they can still be effective and valuable executives with the new management team. Remember that a son or daughter needs the same review and training as any other employee. Just because they are family, doesn't mean they have the necessary skills at the present time to do the job you desire.

Your Turn   *Answer the following:*

► List the top five qualifications for your successor.

Measuring Management Performance

These management divisions were derived from texts in the fields of business management and public service administration and are factors used in employee assessment for hiring and evaluation.

▶ *Leadership:* A leader has the ability to direct people toward a common goal using experience, training and creativity. A person in a leadership position plans for the future while monitoring current activities. A leader is willing to be accountable for decisions made on behalf of others.

▶ *Technical ability:* Technical ability is the combination of training and experience that provides an understanding of how the enterprise is operated in service delivery and production management.

▶ *Management performance:* Management performance is the expression of the day-to-day administrative duties and responsibilities for evaluating short- and long-term business goals. Besides the specifics of everyday issues, a good manager understands the broad view of the business and keeps its future paramount at all times.

▶ *Personal strengths:* Character is what allows someone to succeed at a particular job and fit into the company. Personal strengths entail the total quality of a person's behavior.

The easiest method of finding these qualities and rating them is by using a standardized format. The entrepreneur fills out the Candidate Rating Scale Overview for each candidate. The form includes such information as the individual's job performance strengths and how these relate to the new job and personal considerations such as the ability to work with others, leadership skills, punctuality and so on. Usually these are traits the entrepreneur has already noticed. For instance, Beth is a great organizer, but she has trouble giving directions to subordinates so that her plans can be carried out. She also puts family and personal time ahead of work time. These are not positive or negative traits, just personality clues that may influence a decision about the individual. See pages 133 and 134 for samples of the Candidate Rating Scale Overview for Wayne and Ron.

Comparison of Candidates

The completed forms for Wayne and Ron reveal that Wayne's age and experience in the cabinet business show both positive and negative attributes for his continuation in management. His smoking and back problems may contribute to problems in the future. He seems to want only a limited command of some phases of the business.

Ron, on the other hand, is young, in good physical condition and a nonsmoker. He brings expertise in sales and management information systems. He also shows enthusiasm and wants to be part of the management team.

Candidate Rating Scale: A

Date: _____

Candidate's Name: Wayne B. _____

Current Position: General Manager _____

Date of Hire: 6/3/1980 _____

Age: 52 _____

General Health: Fair, smokes and has trouble with past back injury
_____
_____

What job performance strengths does the candidate now possess:
Well-known in community, knows production techniques, good
relations with suppliers, truly committed to company
_____

Which of these strengths enhances employment status: Wayne is
valuable for his contacts, looks out for business
_____

Personal considerations about the candidate *(hunches, impressions,
thoughts, feedback from others, etc.)*: Wayne learned from the ground up.
He has little interest or knowledge in internal management issues like
finance. Unfamiliar with computers. Not very interested in new ideas
about sales.
_____

Candidate Rating Scale: B

Date: _____

Candidate's Name: Ron L. _____

Current Position: Sales _____

Date of Hire: 9/3/1992 _____

Age: 37 _____

General Health: Energetic, former high school athlete, does not _____ smoke, some alcohol, not abusive _____

_____

What job performance strengths does the candidate now possess:
Ron has a background in sales and has managed a sales force of 8.
Is current on computer applications.

_____

Which of these strengths enhances employment status: Sales, _____
management of employees and MIS

_____

Personal considerations about the candidate *(hunches, impressions, thoughts, feedback from others, etc.)*: Ron has been a good friend and _____ confidant. He is interested in my plan to expand business and find a general manager.

_____

_____

Rating of Business Management Categories

The Management Performance Rating Scale was developed to assess an individual for succession in each of the business management categories. A separate form is used for Wayne and Ron on *management performance, leadership, technical ability and personal strengths* (see figures on pages 137–140). Each category is rated on a scale of one to 10, with a 10 being the best or most prepared and a one representing little or no preparedness at this time. Each management category is broken into its component activities. For example, in leadership each candidate is rated in independence, competitive spirit, handling of pressure, delegation of authority, taking risks, adaptability and accountability. Once the ratings are completed, a total score is computed for each management category. Examine all ratings and determine how each candidate stands with the others. An overall score may be used to make your decision now. Alternately, your assessment will help you see weaknesses in the preparation level of the candidate, which will provide a basis for developing training plans for each person.

An analysis of Wayne and Ron revealed some interesting results for Robert. Ron scored higher than Wayne on leadership and personal strengths. Wayne scored highest on management performance and technical ability. When comparing the two on the self-control category of personal strengths, Robert knew Ron was even-tempered and under control, while Wayne on occasion had been known to yell at employees and use abusive language with suppliers. Robert's preference for behavior on this issue is for the people around him to be in control and treat problems as business issues rather than as personal confrontations.

When comparing the management performance scale, Wayne obviously has more experience than Ron. This doesn't mean, however, that Ron can't learn the required skills for competent management of the business and that Wayne can learn proficiencies in his areas of weakness.

Risk Taking

One last example of the differences between Wayne and Ron is in the risk-taking unit of leadership. Wayne is rated a six and Ron a nine on the forms included here. The difference in the ratings possibly has more to do with age between the two candidates than anything else. Wayne doesn't have a vision of how the company can be used as a springboard for other ventures. Robert believes Ron has that capability. Wayne could possibly improve in his lack of vision through a greater understanding of how a manager's risk-taking is diminished over time. Robert will have to evaluate whether his preference of Ron over Wayne would be influenced by Wayne's willingness to participate in extended training.

After Wayne and Ron have been rated regarding their personal level of performance in each division, Robert must develop a strategy to bring each person to a desired level of expertise within a given time. Robert must also define each operating function of the business so he can define the areas on which to measure Wayne and Ron.

Management Performance Rating Scale

Rate each candidate on a scale of 1 to 10. This scale represents the scope of ability and preparedness of each candidate on the values listed below. A 10 represents the best or most prepared, a 1 represents no value or no preparedness at this time.

	WAYNE	RON
Creative use of resources	1_7_10	1_5_10
Competence	1_9_10	1_5_10
Peer relations	1_8_10	1_6_10
Meets company standards	1_8_10	1_5_10
Accepts feedback	1_8_10	1_5_10
Protects company assets	1_7_10	1_5_10
Planning (short-term)	1_6_10	1_5_10
Planning (long-term)	1_6_10	1_5_10
Evaluation of personnel	1_8_10	1_8_10
Total score	**66**	**51**

Date: _____

Candidate's Name: _____

Leadership Rating Scale

Rate each candidate on a scale of 1 to 10. This scale represents the scope of ability and preparedness of each candidate on the values listed below. A 10 represents the best or most prepared, a 1 represents no value or no preparedness at this time.

	WAYNE	RON
Independence	1_8_10	1_8_10
Competitive	1_8_10	1_9_10
Handles pressure well	1_8_10	1_8_10
Delegates authority	1_6_10	1_9_10
Gives credit when due	1_6_10	1_8_10
Risk taker	1_6_10	1_9_10
Adaptability	1_5_10	1_8_10
Accountability	1_7_10	1_8_10
Total score	**54**	**67**

Date: _____

Candidate's Name: _____

Technical Ability Rating Scale

Rate each candidate on a scale of 1 to 10. This scale represents the scope of ability and preparedness of each candidate on the values listed below. A 10 represents the best or most prepared, a 1 represents no value or no preparedness at this time.

	WAYNE	**RON**
Academic preparation	1_6_10	1_7_10
Understands industry standards	1_8_10	1_5_10
Broad knowledge of products and service	1_10_10	1_5_10
Technical problem solver	1_10_10	1_7_10
Pay attention to detail	1_7_10	1_8_10
Writing skills	1_6_10	1_9_10
Understands MIS	1_6_10	1_10_10
Controls job costs	1_8_10	1_4_10
Total score	**61**	**55**

Date: _____

Candidate's Name: _____

Personal Strengths Rating Scale

Rate each candidate on a scale of 1 to 10. This scale represents the scope of ability and preparedness of each candidate on the values listed below. A 10 represents the best or most prepared, a 1 represents no value or no preparedness at this time.

	WAYNE	**RON**
Ambitious	1_9_10	1_9_10
Broadminded	1_7_10	1_9_10
Capable	1_8_10	1_8_10
Honest	1_8_10	1_8_10
Imaginative	1_7_10	1_8_10
Intelligent	1_8_10	1_8_10
Logical	1_7_10	1_8_10
Self-controlled	1_7_10	1_8_10
Total score	**61**	**66**

Date: _____

Candidate's Name: _____

Management Functions

1. **Management Information System (MIS)**
   This management unit develops databases for payroll, tax reports, inventory control, daily invoicing, statements, cash balances and income statements.

2. **Sales**
   This unit includes geographic boundaries, goal setting and training.

3. **Dispatch**

   This function normally keeps records of deliveries, controls rolling stock, schedules work for the next day or delivery routing.

4. **Accounting**
   This unit usually oversees the MIS department and will produce all needed reports for management for fiscal decisions. This includes making and preparing tax reports, managing receivables and payables.

5. **Office Management**
   This area handles the management and decisions of all internal paper flow. It provides the organization of personnel through which all internal business is conducted.

6. **Field Services**
   The field services unit manages the people in the field who perform a service or produce a product. It is responsible for meeting a schedule, completing a job and quality control.

7. **Equipment**
   This unit conducts maintenance functions on a regular basis to all company equipment. This may be combined with other tasks in the company.

8. **Manufacturing Supervisor**
   This unit is responsible for getting work done on the production floor. It includes scheduling production, handling quality control and maintaining workforce levels.

Robert said he was comfortable with the ratings of Wayne and Ron on the management scales. He was ready to take the next step to develop training opportunities for each of them. He had decided not to announce his choice of successor for some time, feeling that these training modules would be beneficial for the company and the two candidates—no matter what he decided to do.

The plan format forms for Wayne and Ron show how Robert developed his plans to bring both candidates to equal competency.

Family Succession Is Protection for Members

Robert studied his completed rating scales for Wayne and Ron, and he wanted Ron to take over in the next two years. He felt that Wayne was good at what he did and has a presence among the customer base—but the problem that kept lingering was that Wayne wasn't *family.* He said he couldn't see Rachel going to Wayne for assistance if something happened to him. But if Ron was in charge he could protect Rachel's interests and he trusted Ron to do the right thing.

This is a hallmark of family business. It's unfortunate in some ways, but often in bad and confusing situations, family will look to their own. Robert might do himself and Wayne a favor if he sat down with him and explained what he wanted to do. It didn't mean Wayne would have no influence in the company, but at least he would know where he stood. If he wanted to make any other move he would have the opportunity with Robert's blessing—but Robert's treatment of him would be fair, and Wayne would have plenty of opportunity to grow with the company.

Robert had reservations about what Wayne would do when told of Robert's plan. "What if Wayne leaves and takes all his customers with him?" he asked.

Wayne might indeed leave—but that's a chance Robert would always live with, anyway. However, Ron manages the sales force and he would work to retain the customer base. If Wayne thinks he could do better for himself on his own, he should probably try it, but if he is a successful part of the current management team and is duly rewarded, it is not likely he'll move on.

Often when there are multiple possibilities for successor, several outcomes can be expected. A self-selection process among the candidates inevitably emerges. Merely the thought of competing will turn some away. This doesn't mean the evaluation process hasn't been instructive—something will be learned about each person. In the matter of brothers, sisters or other relatives vying to achieve the president's chair, the process may bring on an unwillingness to interfere with family relationships. For some, it may be too sensitive to gamble on winning, only to lose friends and family.

After the evaluation process has been completed, it needs only to be updated or maintained periodically. For Robert, it means he does the hard work early in the process. He then needs to check at the end of six months to see if everything is on track. A regular review of Wayne and Ron may reveal that Ron's preparation is improving at an accelerated pace. He knows that the training provided will benefit the company in many ways. Not only will Wayne and Ron be a better-equipped executive team, but their contributions will enhance the company's productivity and profitability.

Plan Format

Candidate's Name: Wayne B.

Management Unit: Management Information Systems (MIS) and Office Management

Rating: 6

Comment

Wayne has resisted learning the range of capabilities of computerization in the company. Wayne appears to have a good command of what goes on in internal operations. However, he doesn't coordinate well the purchasing and accounting functions to plan material purchases.

Plan Goal

Within two years Wayne needs to have at least an "8" rating. Outcome of training is to prepare him for getting in and out of data banks and using information for short- and long-term planning. Wayne needs to implement a new purchasing scheme that will eliminate storage of materials longer than 30 days to preserve cash supplies. The suppliers can manage next-day delivery.

Plan Strategies

1. Wayne needs to read more management and technical materials. Give him time every month to read trade and management journals on the job.
2. Local community college sponsors weekend workshops on information system training once per semester. Wayne to attend at least one.
3. Occasionally wood laminate suppliers will hold national meeting. Computer applications workshops offered. Make these available to Wayne.
4. Wayne could benefit from spending one-half day per week working with accounting, sales, payroll, etc., learning their tasks for background and cross-training.

Plan Format

Candidate's Name: Ron L.

Management Unit: Field Services

Rating: 5

Comment

Ron has only rudimentary knowledge of how cabinets are manufactured and installed. It is essential for him to learn this craft in order to price the product competitively or offer customer service.

Plan Goal

Ron needs to be rated at "8" or above in proficiency within 18 months. Having him close to Wayne's capability will take a big commitment, but is necessary.

Plan Strategies

1. Ron needs to spend one day per week with hands-on experience in the manufacturing shop until he is satisfied that he can perform most jobs, if necessary.
2. Management should make available to Ron time and opportunity to attend industry-related training opportunities given by suppliers and others in the business.
3. Company time should be made available to Ron to read journals and periodicals related to services.
4. Ron needs to learn methods for installation of cabinets by spending time with the dispatcher to schedule installation jobs and go to the job site to observe installation methods.

"All right," Robert said, "what do I do when I get ready to make my move into other ventures?"

"Once you've established your time to change, review your succession plan. If you see that your successor is still deficient in some areas, talk with the person before you make your move. The measure of their competency is that they can perform the tasks of your job without your assistance. Maybe they're not 100% proficient in some areas, but may become confident as they gain experience and responsibility."

The stages of a successful succession plan are as follows:

1. Review your documentation to date. Make needed changes. Decide who will succeed you.

2. Decide the parameters of the offer to your successor, including financial, legal and personal considerations.

3. Inform your choice and begin to detail your schedule for departure.

4. Make public your decision, letting your employees know first and then your customers.

5. Contact your major suppliers.

6. Plan a public announcement with a celebration.

These steps will allow a simple and dignified passing of leadership.

One last part of this plan should be how the owner-manager wishes to relate to the company after the transfer of leadership. Many owners prefer to continue to consult, others place themselves on the board of directors, or remain president of the company for atime to facilitate the passing of authority.

Summary

Robert wanted to move on to other things, but he needed to find someone he trusted with the family business in his absence. we examined the capabilities of Wayne, the general manager, and Robert's brother-in-law, Ron, as his candidates of choice. After rating them on our management scales, Robert decided that each candidate had distinctive strengths and weaknesses. The next step was to determine each person's readiness to operate the company. Following this was the development of training programs for each to bring them to equivalent competencies.

Robert also revealed that what he really wanted was to advance his brother-in-law, because he was most comfortable keeping the authority with a family member. He decided to tell Wayne and pursuade him to remain on the management team. He is waiting for this decision. Robert will then announce his choice and implement his plan.

Checklist

❏ The goal of succession planning is to find or prepare someone to do your job without your assistance.

❏ Have a confidant in personal and business matters.

❏ In management of any domain, leadership is the most important quality.

❏ Keep a brief profile of key employees and update them regularly for succession candidacy.

❏ When comparing succession candidates, don't be surprised if the one in which you are most interested has some major weaknesses.

❏ Continuous training for succession candidates will benefit both the employee and the company.

❏ Write down your thoughts about your succession candidates.

❏ Once the succession plan is completed, it needs to be updated or maintained only periodically.

❏ You may want to keep a presence with the company while the transition takes place or have a role after.

ASK YOURSELF

► Describe the process you will use to qualify and rate candidates to succeed you.

► Discuss your comfort level with succession planning.

► Discuss the possible factors that influence your selection of a successor.

► Describe the process you and your successor will use to work together during the transaction.

CHAPTER
TEN

CONCLUSION
OF THE
STORY

FAMILY BUSINESS AS AN ADVENTURE IN GROWTH

Robert entered my office uncertain about joining the family business. He wasn't sure he could handle the responsibility of managing a business on his own. At the bank he had become accustomed to most resources being provided for him. He never had to worry about paying rent on his office, collecting money or laying off employees. Even though he was a dedicated loan officer, he still had to perform to his supervisor's expectations. At this point the question uppermost in his mind was, "Can I do it?" Robert had no idea of all the issues and problems he was to find along the path to ownership.

Over time, he showed a great deal of maturity and growth. In the beginning, the biggest hurdle Robert had to overcome in the transition from employee to employer was his concern about his Uncle Jim. This incident called for independent decision making but caused him personal anguish about family involvement. He knew that if he made a big mistake with this problem, it would take a longer time to gain his employees' respect. Robert's success gave him confidence to address issues with Wayne and the rest of the family.

Robert faced major problems in asserting control with Wayne, but these seemed manageable compared to the resolution of the demands made by his Grace, Janis and Rachel. Wayne's personality was that of a long-term employee, who had learned over the years that it would be necessary to act tough to get what he wanted. Somewhat of an opportunist, Wayne felt justified in manipulating Grace to assert his role in the family cabinet company.

It was important that Robert assert his control of the company right away, which meant that he needed to win Wayne's support. At that point Robert realized he knew very little about building cabinets or how to run a small business on his own, but he soon understood that it was more important to have Wayne on his side than to isolate him. Once Robert learned how to be a leader, he could take the time to become a competent manager.

Even though Robert had purchased Grace's share of the company stock, he would have to keep his mother involved with the business. With family, many personal factors conflict with sound business practices. While Grace's involvement was far from ideal in Robert's viewpoint, as a son he also had to consider what was best for her. The strain of adjusting to her husband's death coupled with the loss of her status in the business could have been disastrous. Robert and Grace designed a compromise that would be in the best interests of both the company and his mother. Robert thought this would allow him the autonomy he needed, while maintaining his mother's support and approval.

It wasn't easy. Robert learned that shared authority, with the development of a board of directors and other family involvement, would also be assets for him as owner of the company. He began to see how many viewpoints could enhance his plans for company growth.

Family businesses are often viewed as a haven for nonproductive family members. Although it may be true in some cases, good business people know that payment without production is unwise. Robert did a good job of sticking to his philosophy of work-for-pay with Janis. Even though she expected to fulfill her personal career needs (because she was a stockholder), her employment didn't occur without an agreement that provided value to the company, too.

When Rachel also wanted to use the company for her own career needs, he was smart enough to realize that her happiness was essential to his own. Without her support for what he was doing, the challenges of family business ownership would just become another job. Finding a solution together for her concerns was a positive approach to decision making. Once the issues were discussed, Robert and Rachel agreed. Rachel found the perfect teaching job and couldn't be happier.

Once Robert got through organizing his management team, he wanted to know how to give them feedback about how they were performing their jobs. We discussed options to evaluate his employees, including Ron and Janis. Robert thought he could make arrangements for Ron, just as he had done for

Janis, but Robert understood that for every advantage he provided a family member, he also had to give the benefit to all other employees. This added to an overall feeling of team work by all the participants in the company.

After eight months, Robert wondered how he could expand the business into other markets, maybe diversify into other profitable areas. If he wasn't there on a daily basis, how could he insure continuity of the company? He realized through succession planning that he really wanted Ron to carry on because he was family. While Ron had every capability to become a good manager, Robert knew that the whole family was the overriding consideration in the far-reaching decision of succession. Wayne was a competent and even desirable manager, but the true test was how Rachel would be treated if Robert were no longer involved.

Once his plan was completed, Robert saw that its value was not only in the future but was useful for assessing Ron and Wayne's contribution to the company. In addition, he also realized that this plan would be available for immediate implementation if he desired.

Robert's situation is a perfect example of how, with guidance, a client can master professional and personal growth. My goal in working with Robert was to assist him through the steps needed to reach a point of confidence where he could respond to any issue in his business. Even though he didn't have the advantage of 20 years in the field, he learned how to hold his own and then finally master the management of his business.

Robert grew from an apprehensive, tentative new entrepreneur to someone in command of his destiny. The maturity he exhibited after eight months was crucial to the success of his family's business.

Suggested Reading

Alcorn, Pat B. *Success and Survival in the Family Owned Business.* New York: Warner Books, 1982.

Gerber, Michael E. *The E Myth.* Harper Business, 1986.

Loughary, Jack, and Ripley, Thereas. *Working It Out Together.* New Directions, 1987.

Pine, Arthur. *Your Family Business.* New York: Poseiden Press, 1990.

Tannen, Deborah. *That's Not What I Meant.* New York: Ballantine Books, 1987.

Warschaw, Tessa Albert. *Winning By Negotiations,* McGraw Hill, 1980.

APPENDIX
A

FAMILY

BUSINESS

RETREATS

GO AWAY TOGETHER

An ideal format for bringing together family business principals to evaluate the year's activities and conduct planning is a business retreat. During a retreat, participants withdraw from daily company endeavors to regroup through relaxation or study with a directed agenda. While this may be accomplished under the leadership of a family member, it is more effective if the agenda is developed and carried out with the assistance of an outside facilitator. This format gives family members time to discuss what is on their minds and interact with each other away from the pressures of the business routine. In this setting, family members can interact on salient issues with the security that any emotional content will be handled professionally.

Weekend retreats have been found to be energizing and productive. One favored format is a three-day weekend allowing time for travel to and from the retreat facility, if necessary. Friday afternoon and Saturday morning are devoted to work sessions while Saturday and Sunday afternoons are open for opportunities to engage in local activities such as golf, hiking, tennis, and so on. A Sunday morning session can be scheduled to review the previous few days' activities.

It isn't necessary to schedule a retreat out of town; however, it is important to consider the value of a new or different setting away from the office to allow for relaxation. It is too convenient to interrupt a meeting at the worksite, and principals find it difficult to justify a period of recreation time away from the office.

The first step in planning a retreat is to find a facilitator who will work with all participants from early planning to completion and follow up. Local universities or community colleges with business administration departments are logical places to contact. The yellow pages will list counselors who may have a specialty in group work or management group planning. This person should work closely with all participants to include their issues in agenda planning.

Meanwhile, a designated individual within the business should take on the role of selecting the location for the retreat. Most facilities have professionals on staff who can help with the details of planning registration, meals and recreational activities. Consider if spouses and other family members are to be included when a site is selected and activities planned.

Once the agenda has been approved and the time for the retreat set, all principal parties should make plans to attend.

It is expected that everyone will participate in the work sessions and contribute to the discussion of the agenda items. It is to be expected that someone will attend with a "hidden" agenda; for example, a daughter or son who wants to discuss succession planning when the owner isn't ready or interested in retirement. Often one unhappy relative wants to make an issue of the division of labor or compensation of family members. These hidden issues usually appear at times when other topics are being discussed, and it's the job of the facilitator to recognize the problems this may create. The discussion leader may schedule this subject for another time or poll the group about whether to continue the topic. Most of the time the issues can be deferred for later discussion.

Ground rules are important and should be established by the facilitator at the beginning of the session on Friday. It should be clear that participants can say whatever they feel about an *issue,* but they cannot be abusive to *others.* For instance, the brother—who perceives that while he earns the same salary as his siblings, is working harder and longer hours—doesn't have the right to an outburst about his frustrations regarding his circumstances. The group may need to be reminded of this rule throughout the retreat. Feelings are legitimate, but using them to attack an unprepared person is unacceptable.

Choose a scribe for each work session. Together the facilitator and the scribe get a good representation of what issues were discussed and what kinds of agreements were reached. At the end of the retreat, the notes of the scribes and facilitator can be used for a report to the group. In the last session, the facilitator can share with them the results gained from the previous sessions. These findings will then be produced in a written report. The purpose of the written report is to help the participants recall each discussion point, where they stand on the issue and who or how the group decided to resolve any outstanding issues.

Sometimes major issues can't be settled at a retreat. The facilitator will need to be watchful about this and build in a period when issues off the agenda will require more time or need additional attention. These may be ideas that can be assigned to a work group that will address the issues throughout the following year. At the next retreat, these issues will then be given priority on the agenda and the work group will take the responsibility to report on their results.

Your Turn

Finding the right facilitator for your business retreat may take some time. Ask friends who are in business for references. Call your local college or community business schools for recommendations. Describe what results you would like from the retreat. This might help narrow the range of professionals who could help. Ask for references and be diligent about following up so you will have a good impression about how your retreat may be conducted. Discuss with the possible facilitators what you want and make your choice accordingly.

ABOUT THE AUTHOR

Marshall W. Northington, Ph.D., is the general manager of his family business. He began working there in 1980 following the sudden death of his father. His initial plan was to spend two years learning the family businesss and then open a counseling psychology practice, remaining only as a consultant to the business. This plan was revised and he spent 11 years running the business. In 1991 he resumed his practice, specializing in family-owned business and career planning.

Northington is a 1966 graduate of the University of Arizona. In 1972 he received his Ph.D. in counseling psychology from the University of Oregon.

NOTES

NOTES

ABOUT CRISP PUBLICATIONS

We hope that you enjoyed this book. If so, we have good news for you. This title is only one in the library of Crisp's best-selling books. Each of our books is easy to use and is obtainable at a very reasonable price.

Books are available from your distributor. A free catalog is available upon request from Crisp Publications, Inc., 1200 Hamilton Court, Menlo Park, California 94025. Phone: (415) 323-6100; Fax: (415) 323-5800.

Books are organized by general subject area.

Computer Series

Beginning DOS for Nontechnical Business Users	212-7
Beginning Lotus 1-2-3 for Nontechnical Business Users	213-5
Beginning Excel for Nontechnical Business Users	215-1
DOS for WordPerfect Users	216-X
WordPerfect Styles Made Easy	217-8
WordPerfect Sorting Made Easy	218-6
Getting Creative with Newsletters in WordPerfect	219-4
Beginning WordPerfect 5.1 for Nontechnical Business Users	214-3

Management Training

Building a Total Quality Culture	176-7
Desktop Design	001-9
Ethics in Business	69-6
Formatting Letters and Memos	130-9
From Technician to Supervisor	194-5
Goals and Goal Setting	183-X
Increasing Employee Productivity	010-8
Introduction to Microcomputers	087-6
Leadership Skills for Women	62-9
Managing for Commitment	099-X
Managing Organizational Change	80-7
Motivating at Work	201-1
Quality at Work	72-6
Systematic Problem Solving and Decision Making	63-2
21st Century Leader	191-0

Personal Improvement

Communications

Small Business and Financial Planning